ASK THE BIBLE GEEK® 2

ALSO BY MARK HART:

Ask the Bible Geek®:
Answers to Questions From Catholic Teens

Blessed Are the Bored in Spirit:
A Young Catholic's Search for Meaning

Ask the Bible Geek® 2

More Answers to Questions From Catholic Teens

MARK HART
THE BIBLE GEEK®

SERVANT
BOOKS

PUBLISHED BY ST. ANTHONY MESSENGER PRESS
CINCINNATI, OHIO

Cover illustration and design by Michael Frazier
Book design by Mark Sullivan

LIBRARY OF CONGRESS CATALOGING-IN-PUBLICATION DATA

Hart, Mark, 1973-
Ask the Bible geek 2 : more answers to questions from Catholic teens / Mark Hart.
p. cm.
ISBN-13: 978-0-86716-766-5 (pbk. : alk. paper)
ISBN-10: 0-86716-766-1 (pbk. : alk. paper) 1. Catholic Church—Doctrines—Miscellanea. 2. Catholic teenagers—Religious life—Miscellanea. I. Title. II. Title: Ask the Bible geek two.

BX1754.3.H37 2007
248.8'3—dc22

2006029032

ISBN 978-0-86716-766-5

Published by Servant Books, an imprint of
St. Anthony Messenger Press.
28 W. Liberty St.
Cincinnati, OH 45202
www.ServantBooks.org

Printed in the United States of America.

Printed on acid-free paper.

07 08 09 10 5 4 3 2

Dedication

To my girls, Hope and Trinity:
May you always look past my sin to see His grace.
May you always find your answers in the Answer.
May you always know that your beauty is within.
May you always trust that Dad tries his best
to show you a love words can't express.
May you always strive to be like your mom,
whose beauty is beyond words.
May you always respect yourselves enough
to wait for a man who will do likewise.
And may our Father in heaven kiss your forehead
each night, years after I have ceased to.

Contents

Chapter Two: Encountering God During Advent and Christmastime

Chapter Three: Encountering God During Lent and Easter

Chapter Four: Encountering God During Ordinary Time

Chapter Five: Encountering God All the Time

Introduction

Have you ever looked at your wrist for the time when you weren't wearing your watch? When we depend on something, it becomes second nature to look to it, even if it's not there.

The same can be said about our faith and about God. We get used to having Him around. The more we look to Him, the more obvious are the times when He is not our focus. And the only way to get to the point where looking to God is second nature is to spend more time with Him.

Can you hear a clock ticking right now? Probably not, as we live in a digital age. Do you know what time it is without looking? Probably, as we're so busy in today's culture that we can't get through a day without a schedule.

When did everyone, teenagers included, get so busy? What happened to sleeping in? What about Saturday morning cartoons and summers spent with the alarm clock unplugged? How come reading a book (never mind actually *finishing* one) is such a luxury? Why is reading God's book so difficult to make part of the daily schedule?

A reality of life is that time is running out. From the moment we are born, our bodies begin to die. That should only be a sad statement if this life is all you think there is. A true Christian knows better.

Many modern-day Catholics are long on intentions and short on fulfillment. "I need to read the Bible more," we say. "I have been meaning to get to confession," we offer. "It's time I make some changes," we admit. And the next step is normally that nothing happens. Intentions are great during prayer, but what about during the rest of our time?

Actions speak louder than words, and in His Word actions speak loudest of all. It's time to make time to take action. Wow, I like that sentence.

How often do you waste time with God? The usual response to such a question is "Never. Spending time with God is not a waste." That's true. Society might see our use of time with God as wasteful, since society frowns on things that are not obviously productive and that lack immediate gratification. So what? It's *great* to spend time with God.

Time is the greatest commodity we have as human beings. From the moment you are conceived, your clock is ticking. Some clocks are wound longer than others; some clocks are stopped short. Time and indeed life itself are gifts not to be wasted.

Since I've become a parent, I have learned more than I can write in one book. One thing that I have learned has changed my life and my relationships forever: *love* is spelled *t-i-m-e.*

Now, there aren't many gifts I can give my kids on a youth minister's salary, but the gift of my time is priceless. Time is more influential than power and more important than money.

Sure, you might want your parents to give you more

money because that means more "toys," but the truth is that toys rust and break and ultimately fail to satisfy. It's time, time in relationships, that changes people's lives. That's why God did what He did: The timeless one entered time and space.

Part of the problem with His entering time at a specific, appointed time in history, however, is that two thousand years later, people are questioning whether it really happened, whether it really matters and whether what He said still "holds up" in the highly technological, culturally savvy and politically correct age of the twenty-first century. But that's part of the beauty of God: Although He entered time, *God is timeless*. And although we still encounter Him in time, His truths for our lives are timeless.

The Bible calls us to make a decision about God. It presents a God who shows His love through relationships over time, time and time again. And the Living Word, then and now, shows us that it's time to change. It's time to invite God into our lives.

We can't afford to waste our time here on Earth, when we should be preparing ourselves (and others) for the timelessness of heaven. We should turn our attention from toys that break to lives that are broken, beginning with our own. We can begin by recognizing God *at all times*: in the difficult times, in the stress of holidays, in the boredom of ordinary days and in the random places within our days. Spending time with God during Mass, adoration, Bible study, prayer group, retreat or holy hour is wonderful. Inviting Him into the less structured, less communal moments of your life is just as essential for spiritual growth.

That's why, after a long time away, I've put together this

second volume of *Ask the Bible Geek®*. I pray it helps at least one soul encounter God more deeply.

You might not have time to sit down and read this book in one sitting; it's probably better anyway if you don't. Keep it next to your Bible, and read it when you want to read it. When it comes to this book, *take your time*. When it comes to *the* Book, God's book, *make the time*.

The fact is that when you read books about God you receive grace, but when you read God's Word you are reading grace itself. Don't ever mistake the two. The words contained in this book should act like an arrow pointing back to His Word.

"God is love" (1 John 4:8), and if love equals time, then encountering God's love requires making the time to do so. When I finally made the time to be more present to God, my life changed in more ways than I can explain. Great gifts from God have come to me, both joyful and sorrowful. I would have missed them entirely had I been too busy to notice them. I'm learning every day how to become more present to the Creator in the face of His creation, and I want to keep learning.

How about you?

Are you present to the times when God is nagging and nudging you? Do you see all the ways that He is moving? Do you hear Him calling your name? Do you feel His hand on your shoulder, pushing you forward or holding you back?

If so, that's great. If not, *it's time* that you did. I hope, in some small way, that this book helps you slow down long enough to encounter God in time, all the time, until the end of time.

Check your watch; the clock is ticking.

Chapter One

Encountering God in Difficult Times

Wishing God's direction came with directions

Why is God interested in you?

Then turning to the disciples he said privately, "Blessed are the eyes which see what you see! For I tell you that many prophets and kings desired to see what you see, and did not see it, and to hear what you hear, and did not hear it."

Luke 10:23–24

SITUATION EXPLAINED

What is Jesus thinking? Why me? Why you?

SOLUTION OFFERED

Certainly there are more talented people on this earth, Lord, so why me?

I cannot count how many times I have uttered the above statement in prayer. Can you relate? Do you ever wonder why Jesus takes an interest in you? Maybe you don't think that He does, but you're wrong.

Whether or not you can see in yourself what He sees in you has no bearing on whether or not God loves you. He does. Your shortsightedness also has no bearing on whether or not He has a plan for you. Once again, He does.

Throughout the centuries there have been people well-suited to follow God and well-equipped to lead people, at least in the opinion of society. But those people were not always the ones whom God chose to speak on His behalf.

Many of our great biblical figures—Joshua, David, Esther, Jeremiah, Mary, John and Timothy—were quite young when God called them. Others were young at heart: Noah, Abraham, Sara, Moses, Ruth, Isaiah and Elijah.

There were talented leaders in the time of Jesus whom He could have chosen to be His followers: educated people who were good speakers, charismatic and holy people. But He chose His group of fishermen, tax collectors and rebels. They weren't perfect, but they were passionate, hardworking and humble.

Why does this matter? Well, because it shows that worldly stature means very little to God. He does not measure our worth by age or by accomplishments. Zip codes, bank accounts, brand names and job titles mean little to Him. He reveals Himself and works through the smallest and meekest people He finds.

The fact that you're reading this book is proof that you are active in your faith walk. That is very cool. God has a plan for you. He is calling you to a mission that only you can fulfill in this world. You have the option of answering it or ignoring it. It's your choice.

You don't have to be the smartest, the funniest, the coolest or the most popular person in order for God to use you; you only need to be willing. God can accomplish more with your imperfections than the world can with its perfections. God does not call the equipped; He equips the called.

Today praise God for your imperfections, for those areas in which you feel that you are lacking. That's right, embrace them. Just because you aren't great at one thing doesn't mean you can't be great at something else, and that may be where God wants to use you this day.

One of my heroes is Blessed Pope John XXIII, who was known for his amazing love and sense of humor. On becoming a bishop he wrote to a friend, "Where there are no horses, donkeys will do." He knew that while he might not be the most handsome or the strongest, God apparently felt he could get the job done. And that was right. He went on to become pope, and he changed the church forever.

Pope John XXIII understood something that I often forget when I am muttering the "Why me, God?" question: God knows exactly what He is doing. He created me.

He created you too, and He thinks the world of you—so much so that He stretched out His arms and died for you. His hope is that you join Him back at home in heaven, but not before you have told others about how much He loves them too.

SALVATION GIVEN

Then turning to the disciples he said privately, "Blessed are the eyes which see what you see! For I tell you that many prophets and kings desired to see what you see, and did not see it, and to hear what you hear, and did not hear it."

Luke 10:23–24

Jesus, thank You for always seeing in me more than I see in myself.

Does anybody understand God?

For the foolishness of God is wiser than men, and the weakness of God is stronger than men.

1 Corinthians 1:25

SITUATION EXPLAINED

Ever wonder why God does the things He does? Why does He allow certain things to happen?

SOLUTION OFFERED

There is one period in my life when I had a real problem with God. I couldn't understand why He made certain things happen in my life. How could a loving God let these things take place?

It was easier to point the finger at God when things went wrong in my life than it was to point the finger at others, at the devil or even (God forbid) at myself. Looking back, the truth is that I was angry because God's will wasn't matching up with *my will*, and I didn't like that. I wanted things my way all the time, no questions asked.

I wanted God to be more of a genie than a creator. When things didn't go my way, no matter the reason, it was easy for me to believe that God didn't love me.

I still need to quit second-guessing the artist. I need to quit trying to be the painter and just be the brush. Maybe this is a lifetime process.

That's the essence of what Saint Paul is trying to get at in this verse to the Corinthians. We can get so wrapped up in our own lives, problems, worries and struggles that we lose sight of the bigger picture, the picture that God, the Creator of all, is painting for us.

This verse reminds me that no matter how smart or self-aware I think I am, my tiny human brain cannot even begin to comprehend the vastness and complexity of God's mind. No Ph.D., no supercomputer, no billion-dollar satellite system, will ever come close to scratching the surface of the wisdom of God.

The beauty of this situation is contained in the second part of the verse. When I'm too shortsighted to see beyond myself and my immediate problems, God is there to share His strength. When I feel as if I just want to quit trying or abandon prayer, He is there. He's wise enough to see through what I want and focus on what I need, even before I realize that I need it.

SALVATION GIVEN

For the foolishness of God is wiser than men, and the weakness of God is stronger than men.

1 Corinthians 1:25

Socrates said, "True knowledge lies in knowing that we know nothing." For a guy who wore a toga all year long, he was actually pretty bright.

Jesus therefore said to him, "Unless you see signs and wonders you will not believe."

John 4:48

SITUATION EXPLAINED

Do you have faith? If seeing equaled believing, Christianity would be easy.

SOLUTION OFFERED

There is something to be said for the power of words, especially God's. *Faith* is one of those words that can be easy to speak about but almost impossible to explain. Words can be that way sometimes.

Certain words sound the same as other words but mean something very different:

I'm sure you have *read* about the *Red* Sea in the Exodus account of Moses' leading the Jews out of Egypt.

And the *prophets* found that there were no *profits* to be made in speaking God's word. Picture it: *mourning* every *morning*, walking around in a *daze* for *days*.

You've heard the story about the birth of Jesus and the manger. It's because of *Him* that we have the *hymn* "O Come, O Come, Emmanuel." Now, be sure to join in that *hymn*, because Saint Augustine said about *praise*, "The person who sings *prays* twice."

I wonder if the Magi were *thrown* when they found the king not on a *throne* but in a manger. I wonder how soon they realized that they were not *there* because of *their presents* but for His *presence*.

The folks on the *scene* at the wedding feast in Cana couldn't believe what they had *seen*. Mary didn't *whine* for the *wine;* she simply informed Jesus of the situation. Though He said it wasn't His *hour,* He would never deny *our* Mother. Jesus *knew* where the *new* wine came from.

The events of Holy *Week* show that Jesus was anything but *weak. Would* you carry the *wood* that our Savior did? His *sole* purpose was your *soul* and those of your brothers and sisters. He said that He would *raze* the temple, and God did *raise* His *Son* under the *rays* of the *sun* that Easter morning. The *sight* at that *site* in the garden was so beautiful that all of the Gospel writers would *cite* it. Jesus is the *One* who *won.*

And now at Mass it's in that ordinary *piece* of bread that you will find your *peace.* We are *wholly* different after Communion: we are *holy* because of Jesus' presence. What happens on that *altar* can *alter* us in ways we cannot imagine.

You see? Words carry meaning and power, and sometimes we need to think about more than their sound.

While God's Word might sound familiar, there is often a deeper meaning that He is trying to communicate to our hearts. Faith is not about what you see with your eyes but what you see with your heart.

Faith in God isn't wrapped up in an extravagant package; it's a simple gift wrapped deep within you and within me. Faith is a gift from God, a gift that speaks to the heart more than to the eyes.

We are no different from the folks back in biblical times. They too saw amazing things that they couldn't explain. Some were open to faith and followed; others weren't and didn't.

You have more faith than you realize; we all do. It is an untapped power source that became imbedded in you during your baptism. Tap into it, and trust in it.

Jesus is our doctor, waiting to heal us; He is the surgeon for our souls. But we are not just *patients* waiting to be *billed.* Through God's grace we gain *patience* so that we can *build* the city of God within the city of man.

SALVATION GIVEN

Jesus therefore said to him, "Unless you see signs and wonders you will not believe."

John 4:48

Have faith in Him. He has faith in you.

By the way, be sure to live a *chaste* life if you want to be *chased* by Mr. or Miss Right.

Are you fearful of what following God might mean?

And Peter had followed him at a distance, right into the courtyard of the high priest; and he was sitting with the guards, and warming himself at the fire.

Mark 14:54

SITUATION EXPLAINED

Have you ever been fearful of totally following God?

SOLUTION OFFERED

Hey, Peter, what was it like to see your best friend get pushed around, mocked, spit on and lied about? Did you make eye contact with the guards or try not to?

What did it feel like to turn your back on God, standing just yards away from Him beside a warm fire? Did you stand in the shadows so Jesus couldn't see you? What did it feel like when He finally looked into your eyes? (see Luke 22:61).

Was it harder to hear the crow of the rooster or to watch the way they treated your God? Was it harder seeing the rock in front of the tomb or knowing that you fled when He seemed to need you most?

The night was freezing cold, the fire burning hot, and there was Peter: lukewarm. He chose to remain safe, a bystander. He was afraid to take a stand, afraid to engage—afraid, period. Although his body was next to a consuming fire, his heart was not aflame with love for Jesus but was consumed only with and by self.

It's easy to shake our heads at Peter's behavior, reaction and failure—easy, that is, until we put ourselves in his sandals.

How many times have I turned my back on You, Lord?

How many times have I had the opportunity to acknowledge You and have not?

How many times have I followed You at a distance?

How many times have I seen You clearly but tried to stand far enough away that You couldn't see me?

How many times have I claimed You as friend but not acted as one?

How many times, Lord, will I abandon You when I need to stand for Your truth?

How many times will I choose to "play it safe" rather than live dangerously for You?

What use do You have for a sinner like me, Lord?

Then the answer comes. He has plenty of use for me (and you).

Not only did Jesus forgive Peter, in spite of his failures, but also He gave him a place of honor as the leader of the early church. Peter was our first pope. It was beside a fire that Jesus once again looked Peter in the eyes and asked him, "Do you love me?" three times (see John 21:15–17).

Not only does God forgive us, but He believes in us, entrusts a mission to us and allows us to participate in His work, even after we've run from Him, even after we've been lukewarm. How great and how powerful is the mercy of God!

If you, like me, have been lukewarm toward Christ, you need to leave the false warmth of the world's fire and experience the fire of the Holy Spirit. That only comes from abandoning the fear of what others might say or do to you. "Draw near to God and he will draw near to you" (James 4:8).

SALVATION GIVEN

And Peter had followed him at a distance, right into the courtyard of the high priest; and he was sitting with the guards, and warming himself at the fire.

Mark 14:54

Lord, set my heart on fire, especially when those around me need warmth.

Do you feel as if no one understands you?

For the sake of Christ, then, I am content with weaknesses, insults, hardships, persecutions, and calamities; for when I am weak, then I am strong.

2 Corinthians 12:10

SITUATION EXPLAINED

Do you ever feel as if you're walking this faith walk alone? Do you feel that no one can relate to what you're going through?

SOLUTION OFFERED

Some days really are more difficult than others, aren't they? You might be thinking, "Yeah, how about some *years?*" That might be true as well. Life is certainly filled with ups and downs. The Christian life can be even more difficult because everyone expects you to be joyful, calm and patient. That can be a real challenge.

Often we have an easier time embracing Jesus' divinity than His humanity. When we pray to Jesus, we picture Him only as God and forget about the fact that He was just as human as He was divine. It's when I forget about Jesus' humanity that I can grow annoyed because my life isn't going right. Sometimes I forget the fact that there isn't a feeling I experience that Jesus can't relate to or understand.

One of the greatest gifts we receive when we read the Bible, beyond the grace that comes from praying the Word of God, is a more intimate appreciation for Jesus' understanding and His humanity. Just ask Him, "Hey, Jesus, do you know what it is like to

- "leave your family and live on your own?" See Matthew 4:13.
- "have one of your best friends die?" Look at John 11:32–33, 35.
- "be homeless?" Matthew 8:20 has that answer.
- "be hungry?" See Matthew 4:2.
- "be despised in your own hometown?" See Luke 4:29.
- "go without sleep?" Look at Mark 4:39 and 14:41.
- "be tempted?" Mark 1:13 tells us that Jesus knew that too.
- "be betrayed by a close friend?" Ouch—Luke 22:48.
- "weep?" See John 11:35.
- "have one of your best friends abandon you and even deny knowing you?" Read any of the Passion accounts: Matthew 27; Mark 14:53–15:39; Luke 23; John 18—19.
- "take the blame for something you didn't do?" Well, see Mark 14:61.

The Lord says, "Yes, I know," to all these questions.

Jesus came to us not only fully divine but also fully human. He was tired, sleepy, angry, sad, lonely, hungry, emotional and annoyed. He was just as human as you and I in all things but sin.

Therefore we can trust that He knows our pains and struggles and knows what we need, precisely because He was there for everything, all of it: the fun, the messes, the happiness, the joys, the trials, the sufferings, the despair, the celebrations. Jesus experienced and took part in it all. He still does.

One of the reasons why Saint Paul is hopeful in this verse is because he trusted that the Lord understood the way he felt. Paul took great comfort in the fact that everything he was going through, as difficult as it was, glorified God. He understood that the weaker and humbler he was, the stronger God would be in him. And the same is true for you and me.

The question is not whether the Lord understands how you are feeling; the question is whether or not you are willing to share those feelings with the Lord in prayer.

Salvation Given

For the sake of Christ, then, I am content with weaknesses, insults, hardships, persecutions, and calamities; for when I am weak, then I am strong.

2 Corinthians 12:10

The Lord was *there for* Paul; *therefore* trust that He will be *there for* you too.

The precepts of the LORD are right,
rejoicing the heart;
the commandment of the LORD is pure,
enlightening the eyes.

Psalms 19:8

SITUATION EXPLAINED

Do you ever get overwhelmed? Do you let it affect your attitude? I try not to let it affect mine, but I have to be honest with you.

SOLUTION OFFERED

Oh, if only...

If only I could start the day excited.

If only I was cheerful every time someone walked into the room.

If only I was really, sincerely grateful for each and every meal.

If only I was more understanding when my loved ones were too busy for me.

If only I could be instantly forgiving when people got mad at me.

If only I would take others' anger or criticism without resentment.

If only I could find complete happiness in just sleeping.

If only I could find more pleasure when riding in my car.

If I could do all of these things, I'd be *almost* as good as my dog.

Now, it's obvious that a dog's life is far simpler than a human's life, but maybe I can learn from that. Sometimes the best and wisest thing we can do in our lives, and definitely in our faith walks, is just to simplify.

The best way to do that is to take a look at ourselves, see what areas of our lives are out of control and then, through prayer, put them into perspective. Doing so ensures that we see those areas not merely through our own points of view but through the Lord's. While dogs are great, it is Christ who is truly "man's best friend." He is that simple, and He wants us to be as well.

He uplifted and perfected the precepts (the laws or teachings) that Psalm 19 speaks about. Christ's law is pure. It is rooted in love and founded on the Golden Rule: "Whatever you wish that men would do to you, do so to them" (Matthew 7:12). Christ's law is one that affirms and challenges us, calling all of us to greater patience, peace and simplicity.

SALVATION GIVEN

The precepts of the LORD are right,
rejoicing the heart;
the commandment of the LORD is pure,
enlightening the eyes.

Psalms 19:8

The next time life has you too stressed, take a lesson from Fido and *go for a walk.*

Are you in pain?

Count it all joy, my brethren, when you meet various trials.

James 1:2

SITUATION EXPLAINED

If God is so loving, why does He let us go through painful times?

SOLUTION OFFERED

My godchild asked me why, if God loves us, does He let us feel pain? My mind scrambled to find a way to explain the purpose of suffering and its role in our salvation to a seven-year-old.

"Well, you like it when your dad picks you up and hugs you, right?" I asked her.

"Yes, I love it," she responded.

Then I asked, "Well, has your dad ever hugged you too tight?"

"Yeah, I don't like it when he does that," she answered.

"But you know that he only hugged so hard because he loves you so much, right?"

I could see that she understood as she smiled and ran to her dad to give him a hug.

This verse from the Book of James tells us to be joyful when we go through trials. Why?

Because trials show that God is at work in our lives. Every struggle in our lives is an opportunity to draw closer to or stray further away from God.

If God has allowed you to suffer in your life, consider it a blessing that He believes in you enough to know that you can handle it. When you keep your eyes on Him through the pain, others notice and see your enduring love for God.

God loves us more than we can comprehend, like any good father. Sometimes He just loves you and me so much that He seems to squeeze a bit too hard.

Look to God in times of trial. He believes in you. The question during suffering is, do you believe in Him?

SALVATION GIVEN

Count it all joy, my brethren, when you meet various trials.

James 1:2

Sometimes when He takes us by the hand, it leaves a scar (see John 20:27).

This is how you are to make it: the length of the ark three hundred cubits, its breadth fifty cubits, and its height thirty cubits. . . . Noah did this; he did all that God commanded him. . . . The waters prevailed and increased greatly upon the earth; and the ark floated on the face of the waters.

Genesis 6:15, 22; 7:18

SITUATION EXPLAINED

What does the blueprint for an ark have to do with living in modern times? More than you might think.

SOLUTION OFFERED

Do you ever open your Bible to or hear at Mass one of those "old school" verses like the one above? They can leave you wondering, "How does this apply to my life?"

Verses like this one are like icebergs: 90 percent of their depth is below the surface.

Now, on the surface, this might just seem like useless information that doesn't make much difference in your twenty-first-century life, with stress from school and work or with strains in relationships. It might leave you wondering what (if anything) God is trying to communicate to you. It's at that point that many dismiss God's Word as outdated or irrelevant, but nothing could be further from the truth.

There is great truth still applicable to the modern life even in these verses. We just have to be willing to do the work, to dig a little deeper.

God is not just the designer of the ark; He's more than the "ark-itect." He's the engineer. He doesn't just tell Noah to build a houseboat. He gives him very explicit instructions for this watercraft.

God gets exact with Noah for one reason: so the ship will

survive the storm. If Noah had ignored God's design and built the boat on his own (like some kind of control freak), he would have slept with the fishes. Instead, as we all know, Noah was faithful, and sunshine followed the storm.

The author of life and the Creator of creation doesn't just give orders; He gives blueprints. If you are suffering and are wondering what God is doing, remember this simple lesson from Noah's life: God knows well what you can take. And while He doesn't cause every raindrop or teardrop in your life, He does allow the storm clouds to roll in and dump on you from time to time. That's not because He doesn't love you or believe in you; it's because He *does*.

God made you; He designed you in the womb (see Psalm 139, Jeremiah 1:4–5). He knows what you can handle. It's usually far more than you think you are capable of handling. The Bible promises us that God doesn't set us up for failure. He wants us to succeed. He never allows us to undergo a trial that is too difficult for us (1 Corinthians 10:13).

The storms of life may have come your way already, or the skies might be sunny in your life right now but you see storm clouds on the horizon. That's not meant to be a "downer" but just the reality of life. But the storms don't have to be as painful as we make them. Storms don't mean God has abandoned us. Often they mean that God believes in us. He knows that if we are faithful and follow His "blueprint," we will survive with flying colors, just like Noah's rainbow. No matter how strong the rain or how high the wave, you'll be riding high when the sun shines again.

If you want to insure your life and the life of your family, do as Noah did: follow God's plan for you, and follow it exactly. You don't know what that plan is? Pray about it, and let Him tell you.

Oh, and be patient: The ark wasn't built overnight. Did you notice the length of that thing? A cubit is between eighteen and twenty-one inches, which means that the ark was over one-and-a-half football fields long. Noah may have been a novice sailor, but he was apparently a patient man.

Like the ark, you are a divine design, and you are made not only to survive but to thrive.

SALVATION GIVEN

This is how you are to make it: the length of the ark three hundred cubits, its breadth fifty cubits, and its height thirty cubits. . . . Noah did this; he did all that God commanded him. . . . The waters prevailed and increased greatly upon the earth; and the ark floated on the face of the waters.

Genesis 6:15, 22; 7:18

Now, whether or not Noah was seasick, that is another question.

Are you depressed?

For you, O Lord, are my hope,
my trust, O LORD, from my youth.

Psalm 71:5

SITUATION EXPLAINED
Don't let depression get you or your loved ones down.

SOLUTION OFFERED
First, if you or someone you know is downcast or suffering from depression, let me say that God cares. I know it may seem as if God is very distant, but remember this: It is often when God seems furthest away that He, in fact, draws closest to us. All we need to do is call out to Him, inviting Him to dwell in our hearts in a new way. He will respond, for He is faithful.

God promised us, "Behold, I am with you always, to the close of the age" (Matthew 28:20). His Scriptures are His love letters to His children, assuring us (especially in times of doubt) of His unending love for us and His continual and eternal presence in our lives.

Everyone goes through down times; they are a part of life. When people nowadays say they are "depressed," it can mean several things—from just sort of "bummed out" all the way down to clinical depression.

I am not a counselor or a licensed therapist, but many counselors I have spoken to and worked with have explained to me some of the signs of serious depression:

- less interest in activities, even enjoyable ones
- significant weight loss or gain
- little appetite nearly every day

- insomnia nearly every night
- fatigue or loss of energy
- feelings of worthlessness or intense guilt
- inability to concentrate
- recurring thoughts about self-harm or suicide

If you are feeling depressed, I encourage you to talk to someone about how you are feeling: a priest, a youth minister, a family member or an adult friend who will understand. Take time to really talk it out with someone you trust.

Also, never be afraid to find and talk to a counselor. Counseling does not make you abnormal, weird or sick; that is a misconception. Sometimes we all need an impartial, outside observer who can help us in our struggles. A good counselor is trained to ask the right questions and listen to your answers. Talking to one can better your chances of finding joy again.

Remember that your life is precious. You are God's child. Anything you're feeling, no matter how hopeless, can be resolved in time. Take an active role: Pray for peace and for healing, and talk to someone who can help you through this time.

If it's a friend who is depressed, don't take his or her situation lightly. It's important that we offer people the healthy attention and encouragement they deserve, at the same time remembering that we (or most of us) are not trained in handling depression on our own. Don't hesitate to suggest professional help.

I can't prescribe medication, but I can "prescribe" some great verses that speak to the heart and bring hope:

- John 14:27
- 1 Peter 1:6–9
- Philippians 4:6–8
- 2 Corinthians 4:8–10
- Psalm 31
- Psalm 138:7
- Isaiah 40:31
- Isaiah 41:10

Take the time to write out or highlight these and other helpful verses in your Bible. God's Word is the best source of hope, better than any "self-help" book you might find at the bookstore.

Salvation Given

For you, O Lord, are my hope,
my trust, O Lord, from my youth.

Psalm 71:5

God loves you, and so do I. Keep praying, and know that I am praying for you, too.

Do you get angry?

The scribes and the Pharisees brought a woman who had been caught in adultery, and placing her in their midst they said to him, "Teacher, this woman has been caught in the act of adultery. . . . Moses commanded us to stone such. What do you say about her?" This they said to test him.... Jesus bent down and wrote with his finger on the ground. And as they continued to ask him, he stood up and said to them, "Let him who is without sin among you be the first to throw a stone at her." And once more he bent down and wrote with his finger on the ground.

John 8:3–8

SITUATION EXPLAINED

Ever have someone really "get under your skin"? What do you do when someone makes you angry?

SOLUTION OFFERED

This is one of the most famous episodes in all of the Gospels. I have heard it preached about, as you probably have, hundreds of times, and there are more meanings and lessons to be taken from it than we could talk about in a couple of pages.

Let's take a simple approach to it this time around. First, read it one more time and pay attention to the details, especially Jesus' actions.

This is one of Jesus' coolest moments. I mean "cool" both as in "Jesus is cool" and as in He "keeps His cool." There are many things our Lord is trying to teach us about judgment, sin, forgiveness, hypocrisy, punishment and mercy.

Beyond all that, though, many times I get caught up in wondering, what *was* He writing on the ground?

31

Theologians have hypothesized about this for centuries, pointing to references from Genesis to Jeremiah to Revelation. Nobody knows for sure, so I have decided to focus not on *what* He was writing but on *why* He was writing. Picture the scene. The Pharisees get in Jesus' face and try to trip Him up. Rather than losing His temper, He pauses and reflects, thinking before He speaks (personal note: I need to learn to do that more often). He bends down, which in the Mediterranean culture was a sign of humility (I need to learn to do that more often, too).

After the Pharisees continue to press Jesus, He speaks very calmly but with conviction and then returns to writing on the ground. He avoids the extreme reaction of being unmerciful or unjust, even though that's the way those around Him are being (I really need to learn to do that more often!).

Jesus gives you and me a great example in this episode:

1. He thinks before He speaks.
2. He models humility in front of others.
3. He shows mercy and justice to those who don't show it back to Him.

All three are easier said than done. Like I said, Jesus is cool on many levels.

Salvation Given

The scribes and the Pharisees brought a woman who had been caught in adultery, and placing her in their midst they said to him, "Teacher, this woman has been caught in the act of adultery.... Moses commanded us to stone such. What do you say about her?" This they said to test him....Jesus bent down and wrote with his finger on the ground. And as they continued to ask him, he stood up and said to them, "Let him who is without sin among you be the first to throw a stone at her." And once more he bent down and wrote with his finger on the ground.

John 8:3–8

Jesus really knew how to live, didn't He? Of course, He is "the way, the truth, and the life" (John 14:6).

What comes out of your mouth?

Jesus, wearied as he was with his journey, sat down beside the well.…The woman said to him, "Sir, you have nothing to draw with, and the well is deep; where do you get that living water?" … Jesus said to her, "Every one who drinks of this water will thirst again, but whoever drinks of the water that I shall give will never thirst."

John 4:6, 11, 13–14

SITUATION EXPLAINED

Doctors tell us that most people need to drink more water. That is good advice, for more reasons than mere hydration.

SOLUTION OFFERED

This passage from the Gospel of John appears very simple on the surface, but like the well that Jesus is sitting next to, it actually runs very, very deep.

You see, back then the well was a very busy place. Each morning when the men went to work, their wives would carry large clay jugs on their heads to the nearest well to get water for their families: for daily cooking, cleaning, bathing and so on. Depending on the size of the family, the wife might have to make several trips each day, continually refilling the three-gallon or so jug, because when filled it could weigh as much as fifty pounds.

But the wives didn't complain; they loved going to the well. Why?

The well was a cultural hotspot, a place where the women would meet with neighbors and *gossip*. (Disclaimer to the women reading this: That doesn't mean that the men didn't gossip, just that they did it in the fields, on the docks or in the marketplace.) Basically, the well in Jesus' time was kind of like the modern-day high school locker room, college common room or office watercooler.

At its core gossip is, truthfully, a very selfish act. It can strip others of their names, reputations and dignity. At the same time gossip usually serves to elevate the stature of those who are doing the talking. People gossip in an effort to make themselves look better or feel better about their lives.

Too often gossip begins with the claim, "Well, I know I shouldn't say it, but it is true." And while it may be true, the question is, "Does it bring God (or the other person) glory?" Does it need to be said?

Jesus chooses this location, the *well*, to demonstrate how the world quenches its desire for attention and exaltation in worldly ways, while true Christians have their thirst (desire for attention) quenched *only* by God, only with the water that leaves us thirstless. But in order to get that water, we need to be willing to go deep ourselves: to look deep within our own well (our heart) at why we say the things we say and why we do the things we do.

What makes this story interesting is that the woman to whom Jesus is talking was a Samaritan, and Jews and Samaritans, as a rule, did not get along. It was in this that Jesus showed what a deep person He really is and what kind of person He calls each of us to be. He wants us to reach out to those "we're not supposed to like" and think twice about the things we say and don't say.

It's often when I'm talking or even joking about others that I get myself in trouble. Of course, I can't talk if I'm drinking water.

Well, well, well. Maybe drinking more water will make me healthier in body *and* soul. It's worth a shot.

SALVATION GIVEN

Jesus, wearied as he was with his journey, sat down beside the well.... The woman said to him, "Sir, you have nothing to draw with, and the well is deep; where do you get that living water?" ... Jesus said to her, "Every one who drinks of this water will thirst again, but whoever drinks of the water that I shall give will never thirst."

John 4:6, 11, 13–14

So when it comes to gossiping, are you doing "well"? If so, keep it up. If not, ask Jesus for a drink of water.

Are you affected by hatred or racism?

Here there cannot be Greek and Jew, circumcised and uncircumcised, barbarian, Scythian, slave, free man, but Christ is all, and in all.

Colossians 3:11

SITUATION EXPLAINED

Ever read a verse like the one above and think to yourself, "Huh?" I do.

SOLUTION OFFERED

Sometimes verses can appear so complicated and so outdated that, if we read them at all, we sort of "gloss over" them. With a bit of background, however, it is amazing how one little verse can really explode with meaning, even in the twenty-first century.

Basically, this verse from Colossians is all about barriers that existed between different races, different cultures and different classes of people. Stick with me here.

You see, Greeks thought that they were "it" and that everyone else (especially those who didn't speak Greek) were "barbarians": uncivilized, uneducated and unworthy to be in the same breathing space or even the same empire. Meanwhile the Jews looked down on all those (Greeks included) who were not Jewish and therefore not God's chosen people.

The Scythians were the lowest of the low, sort of the "barbarians of the barbarians." Everyone else considered them to be not much more civilized than wild beasts. Further, slaves back then weren't even considered human beings but more like "living tools" of a landowner. They had no rights whatsoever.

Then along came Jesus Christ, the revolutionary from a podunk area called Nazareth. His heart-piercing and eye-opening message brought down all of these cultural, racial and geographic barriers. Jesus was the constant, the "least common denominator," if you will, and a very unexpected one at that.

Through Christ this Scripture verse has an incredible and deeply convicting message, even in today's culture. Jesus teaches us some things about man-made barriers:

• Christianity extends beyond you, your nationality or the beliefs of your birth family.

• People who normally would have killed one another because of the color of the other's skin or because of the other's hometown now sit at the same table and break bread together, with one common Eucharistic Prayer. Racism dies in Christ.

• Christianity destroys ritualistic barriers, as both the circumcised and the uncircumcised are invited to find oneness in their Christian beliefs, in their Creed. Christianity is one family and one faith. Personal issues die in Christ.

• The cultured and the uncultured have a common ground in the liturgy (the Holy Mass), a place where the most scholarly and the least educated are equally important and can worship together. Vanity and pride die in Christ.

• The class system ceases to exist, as slaves and their masters pray side by side, offering a sign of peace to one another, no longer separated by society's standards. Social distinctions and worldly cares all die in Christ.

If we are truly Christian, then we are called to model this type of barrier-breaking mentality. We must build a community that sees human worth even in places and in people where it is not seen normally.

Racism is not of Christ. Inequality is not of Christ. Even cliques are not of Christ.

Anything that makes the person next to you feel less a person is not of Christ. May we never be part of that cause but always part of the solution.

God loves you very much, as well as the people whom you find really difficult to love. They might not know it or believe it yet. With your forgiving example, though, one day they just might.

It's easy to dislike. It's easy to hate. Loving, now, that is tough.

SALVATION GIVEN

Here there cannot be Greek and Jew, circumcised and uncircumcised, barbarian, Scythian, slave, free man, but Christ is all, and in all.

Colossians 3:11

Barriers are man-made, but remember what we profess in the Creed: Jesus was "begotten, not made." Man-made barriers have no power over Christ.

Do peers pressure you?

And if a blind man leads a blind man, both will fall into a pit.

Matthew 15:14

SITUATION EXPLAINED

Are you a leader or a follower?

SOLUTION OFFERED

Leading is not easy. Leading requires that a person "put himself out there," take a stand and refuse to look back.

Look at the conductor of an orchestra, for instance. For conductors to lead, what must they do first? They must *turn their backs* on the crowd.

It's the same in our faith lives. If I want to be a true leader, a true "conductor" for Christ, then I need to be willing to turn my back on the crowd and turn my eyes, attention and soul to Him fully.

This verse from Saint Matthew talks about "the blind leading the blind." Did you know that this phrase came directly from Christ? It raises an interesting question for me: Throughout most of the day or most of the week, am I a leader or a follower?

A true leader doesn't follow public opinion. A true leader doesn't surrender to peer pressure. True Christians nowadays are leaders, whether or not they set out to be, because to be a Christian means to stand and defend the truth, no matter the personal cost.

True Christians are more concerned with Christ than with the crowd. True Christians would rather be unpopular in friends' eyes than unpopular in the eyes of God. True Christians fight the temptation to take the easy way out; they stand for Christ.

SALVATION GIVEN

And if a blind man leads a blind man, both will fall into a pit.

Matthew 15:14

To be a true "conductor," I probably should start with my own *conduct*.

Chapter Two

Encountering God During Advent and Christmastime

Finding His presence under the tree

What's the deal with Advent?

Where shall I go from your Spirit?
  Or where shall I flee from your presence?

Psalm 139:7

SITUATION EXPLAINED

Do you ever play hide-and-seek with God? I know I do.

SOLUTION OFFERED

Hide-and-seek was my favorite game growing up. The strategy of securing the perfect hiding place, the frantic scurry to hide, the thrill of the count, holding my breath as I heard the seeker getting closer—it was almost too much pressure for my little heart to take.

The lessons learned in hide-and-seek are lessons we can carry with us throughout life: the ability to think under pressure, the integrity to not look while counting, the self-control in remaining silent for long periods of time as well as the pure joy of playing a game with friends, just to name a few.

Too often, however, I treat my relationship with God like a game of hide-and-seek. I run and try to hide from Him (as if He cannot see me!). At times I even hold my breath and don't talk to Him. I figure that if He can't find me, He can't ask me to change.

There's just one problem with that thought process: We can't hide from God.

To God everything is exposed: all of our faults, imperfections, personal secrets but also all of our talents, traits, successes and achievements—that's the good news. The even better news is that God is always seeking you and me.

"For the Son of Man came to seek and to save the lost" (Luke 19:10).

That is one of the reasons why the church gives us the season of Advent. Over the four weeks preceding Christmas, we prepare *not just* for Jesus' coming as a baby in a manger but also for His Second Coming. The word *Advent* means "to come," and the church, with great wisdom, nudges us with a "wake-up call" to ensure that we are honest with our God and in right relationship with Him before He comes again.

God is seeking you. Are you hiding from Him? If not, good. If so, stop. You have no reason to hide yourself from Him.

He loves us even more than we love ourselves, so let Him. He's coming back at some point. That fact is only scary if we're not where we need to be in relationship to God. A relationship with Jesus is all fun without any of the games.

Advent is a beautiful gift, so seek God and make the season one of depth and of honesty. Expose your soul before God, and allow Him to love you for who you truly are: a sinner in need of His mercy, a work in progress.

As hide-and-seek reminds us, "ready or not, here He comes."

SALVATION GIVEN

Where shall I go from your Spirit?
Or where shall I flee from your presence?

Psalm 139:7

There's no need to hide when it is God that you seek.

How much can you accomplish in one second?

For everything there is a season, and a time for every matter under heaven.

Ecclesiastes 3:1

SITUATION EXPLAINED

Some things only take a second of your time.

SOLUTION OFFERED

Time is a tricky thing. There is always too much of it when you're waiting and never enough when you need it. It moves too slowly when you're young and too fast when you're old.

Of course, we are the ones who struggle with time. God is timeless. He doesn't get impatient the way we do, and He doesn't worry about having enough time for what He wants to accomplish.

Each year millions of college students wish Christmas were already here, so exams would be over. Likewise, many employees are longing for the vacation days Christmas brings. On the other hand, busy shoppers can find the countdown to Christmas a little unnerving. Christmas can't arrive quickly enough for some, while others would like a little more time to prepare.

But whether people are ready or not, excited or dismayed, Christmas Day comes and then, poof, it's all over. All that preparation, all that shopping, all that cleaning, all that cooking, all that wrapping, all that traveling, all that busyness, comes to a close in the blink of an eye. We're left with a sink full of dishes, trash cans full of wrapping paper, bellies full of food and a mailbox full of bills.

Unfortunately for many people, Christmas is just an event, like homecoming or prom. It brings lives together but seldom changes them. It's another twenty-four-hour day, with its seconds, minutes and hours rolling into one another.

A second doesn't seem like much. Heck, there are 86,400 seconds every day. But it only takes *one second* to have your life turned upside down by the Lord. Just a one-second encounter with God is all you need to be eternally altered, forever changed.

Time doesn't play favorites. One second can bring joy as easily as it can bring pain. In one second hearts can stop and hearts can start beating. In one second screeching tires either stop or keep moving. In one second chastity can be defended or relinquished. In one second a gun can fire or a finger can fall from the trigger. In one second a person can say, "I'm sorry," or remain silent. In one second a baby's life is protected or taken by his mother. In one second a couple can say, "I do," or walk out. In one second we can turn our hearts to God or to ourselves. In just one second we can change the course of our history and maybe someone else's.

In one second an angel's light surrounded a teenage girl.

In one second Jesus' tiny heart began beating within the Virgin Mary.

In one second Joseph's fears became secondary.

In one second a guiding star appeared in the sky.

In one second water turned into wine.

In one second Peter walked on water.

In one second Lazarus breathed again.

In one second Jesus gasped His final breath.

In one second His heart beat again.

God can change your life in *one second* if you let Him. You'll have 86,400 chances for Him today if you stay up (only 43,200 if you sleep really, really late). Like those who have gone before you, you probably don't know where God is leading you, but that's OK. Let Him lead.

And if you feel that letting Him lead has burned you in the past, open yourself up again and give God that *second* chance. It's about time.

SALVATION GIVEN

For everything there is a season, and a time for every matter under heaven.

Ecclesiastes 3:1

A life lived for Christ is second to none.

Why are holidays so important?

This is the day which the LORD has made;
let us rejoice and be glad in it.

Psalm 118:24

SITUATION EXPLAINED
Every day is a holy day.

SOLUTION OFFERED
As many of you probably know, the word *holiday* is actually an Old English derivation of "holy day." The two expressions "holiday" and "holy day" are intimately linked.

In a way every day is a holiday because every day is holy. What does this mean?

It means that we are called to celebrate each day as if it were Christmas. We are called every day to reflect and be thankful as if it were Thanksgiving, and we are called to joyfully proclaim Christ's resurrection as if it were Easter Sunday.

It means that:

- every day we should tell folks in our lives how much they mean to us;
- every day we should be thankful for our blessings and the gift of life;
- every day we should be sure to exercise and to get some rest;
- every day we should pick up the phone and talk to someone we haven't seen for a while;
- every day we should smile and greet those whom we meet on the street;
- every day we should take time to reflect on our past and look with hope to the future;

• every day we should hold our loved ones close.

And most importantly, it means, as the verse reminds us, that no matter what happens, whether it is a great day or whether things just don't seem to go our way, we can take comfort because God is in control and He will take care of His own. He takes care of those who believe in Him. He loves you.

SALVATION GIVEN

This is the day which the LORD has made;
let us rejoice and be glad in it.

Psalm 118:24

The *Son* is shining. Rejoice. Because a day without sunshine is, well, night.

Why does Mary get such props?

And behold, you will conceive in your womb and bear a son, and you shall call his name Jesus.

Luke 1:31

SITUATION EXPLAINED

Some people feel that God is less appreciated or loved when we honor the Blessed Mother. Does an artist feel unappreciated when we praise him for the work of his hands? Do parents feel unloved when we are touched by their child's life?

SOLUTION OFFERED

When Mary awoke that morning and began her daily chores, do you think that she dreamed she would be visited by an angel? As she walked to the well, maybe speaking with friends about her upcoming wedding to Joseph, do you think that she could fathom the turn her life would take? As she lay down on the mat in her home that night and offered her evening prayers, do you think she had an inkling of how beautiful or of how difficult her life would turn out to be?

We have the benefit of looking at Mary in hindsight, and that view can get skewed. We know the Blessed Virgin Mary as the Mother of God, early church disciple, faithful saint, wife and mother and the Queen of Heaven. We often forget about the humble teenage girl whose life was changed in an instant, and who changed our lives forever, with her simple *yes* to life.

By "life" I don't just mean her willingness to give birth to the Messiah. I mean her *yes* to all that life carries with it, on a daily basis.

Everyone searches for "the meaning of life." Life, though, is not something to be found; it is something to be experienced. It is given by God, not taken from Him. Life can be described as a search for truth, in which we deal with pain, yearn for true love, remain hopeful for good outcomes, often fear the unknown and usually don't like to sacrifice.

What happens within that search? Sometimes the truth, the pain, the outcome, the fear, the sacrifice and even the love seem more than you and I can bear. But Mary bore all of these things when she bore Him, so that He might bear fruit in us and we might bear fruit in this world.

Mary didn't bear Jesus to "bore" us. She bore Him to bring life. She didn't know what would happen next; she just said yes to God and then kept saying yes to Him with every turn. She opened her hands and heart and said, "Take me where you want to take me.... Let it be to me according to your word" (see Luke 1:38).

Life takes on a different meaning when we welcome Jesus' divinity as Mary did. Through the divine eyes of God, we view our lives from a timeless point of view, not from a temporary human perspective. People will view your life much differently two thousand years from now, for instance, from the way you presently view it. They might not see the hardships you are going through. We do the same when we look at biblical figures, in particular our mother Mary.

You will know the hardships, and so will God. You will also know the love and happiness from God. And you will have a choice, maybe even today (though probably not with an angel), to answer and follow God's call for you.

The choice you will make, *that* is life.

SALVATION GIVEN

And behold, you will conceive in your womb and bear a son, and you shall call his name Jesus.

Luke 1:31

The life God gives us is only too much to bear when we try to bear it without the one who gives it.

Are you "set" for the Nativity?

And going into the house they saw the child with Mary his mother, and they fell down and worshiped him.

Matthew 2:11

SITUATION EXPLAINED

You might want to sit in front of a Nativity set and pray. After all, you are a part of it.

SOLUTION OFFERED

You may have a Nativity set beneath your Christmas tree or on a table in your house. There is almost certainly one on display somewhere in or around your local church.

Saint Francis of Assisi is credited with being the first person to create a Nativity scene. He used live people and animals to bring the birth of Jesus "to life" in 1223. And that's the coolest part of Saint Francis' Nativity scene: It was a "living Nativity."

That's not to say that statues, figurines and pictures are not useful or effective. Works of art help us visualize and focus our minds in prayer. They're especially useful to those of us who have a difficult time concentrating. It's not that we worship the wood or paint, obviously; they're just tools to help us enter more deeply into prayer.

The Nativity scene is not something simply to be admired or to be stared at. It's not just something that we reflect on. The Nativity scene is something that we, as Christians, are supposed to enter into; it is something that we do enter into as Catholics during every Mass.

Christ comes right into our midst in a unique way at the Mass. He enters this sinful world with the beautiful simplicity and humility of a baby. You and I are characters not only in God's story and plan of salvation history but within the living Nativity scene at each Mass.

The Holy Mass is not a "performance"; it is Jesus' coming right into the midst of our lives and calling us near to Him. It is Jesus' looking us right in the eyes. The Nativity and the Mass are about Christ's presence among us and our reaction to Him and His truth.

Who are you in the living Nativity scene at your church? Which character do you most resemble?

I look at my Nativity set and realize that at one point or another, I've felt like just about every character I see there.

Sometimes I proclaim Christ's presence with passion and authority, as did the angel.

Sometimes I bow before Christ, offering Him my gifts, as did the "wise guys."

Sometimes I seek Jesus and just sit, humbly gazing at His wonder, as did the shepherds.

Sometimes I feel like the star that says nothing, but exists to point toward Christ.

Sometimes I feel like the hay, getting trampled and stepped on by everyone around me.

Sometimes I see Christ's truth as something in this world that I'd do anything to protect, just as Saint Joseph did.

Sometimes I am so close to Christ that I can almost feel the joy of His birth or the pain of His death, as the Blessed Virgin Mary did.

Sometimes I am so awkward around Christ that I feel like the ox.

And then there are the times that I'm stubborn and stupid around Christ. That's when I feel like the donkey.

How about you? The character you relate to can change from year to year, day to day and hour to hour, because life, like the Nativity scene and like the Mass, is meant to be experienced, not just observed.

Who are you today in relation to Jesus? Who do you want to be? Who is He calling you to be? Because the fact is that, just like every person and animal in that set, He wants you close to Him. He always has and He always will.

SALVATION GIVEN

And going into the house they saw the child with Mary his mother, and they fell down and worshiped him.

Matthew 2:11

At Mass you become a walking manger (a tabernacle), as Christ rests and breathes within you.

Just how little is this town of Bethlehem?

But you, O Bethlehem,...
from you shall come forth for me
    one who is to be ruler in Israel....
He shall stand and feed his flock in the strength of the LORD,
    in the majesty of the name of the LORD his God.
And they shall dwell secure, for now he shall be great
    to the ends of the earth.

Micah 5:2–4

SITUATION EXPLAINED

So we've all sung about it before, but what's the big deal about Bethlehem?

SOLUTION OFFERED

The hymn "O Little Town of Bethlehem," composed in 1867, is one of the most famous Christmas songs ever written. Have you ever stopped to listen to the words you're singing? Do you know what makes this town so important?

This Scripture was uttered by Micah, one of the minor prophets who lived around 750 BC. That means that he prophesied (foretold) that the Messiah's (Jesus') birthplace would be Bethlehem, and he did it over seven hundred years before Mary went into labor. That's pretty impressive, huh?

Here are a few more interesting facts for any fellow "Bible geeks" out there. Maybe they'll help the song carry new meaning when we sing it from now on:

Bethlehem is a small town in hill country about five miles south of Jerusalem, and it stands about 2,550 feet above sea level (that's about half a mile).

The name "Bethlehem" literally means "house of bread"; it seems a fitting birthplace for the "bread of life" (John 6:48), doesn't it?

It's the town where David was born and was crowned King of Israel. Don't forget, David was Jesus' great, great great grandfather.

Today Bethlehem goes by the Arab name Beit-Lahm, which has been translated "house of flesh" (another interesting twist, given John 6:51–58).

None of these facts are as important as the fact that Bethlehem is the birthplace of our Lord. This is where a king, *the King,* entered the world—not on a throne made of gold but in a box made of wood. Hundreds of years earlier Micah probably didn't know how the story would end.

Neither did the witnesses at Jesus' birth. Who would have thought, on that quiet, peaceful night beneath the star-filled sky, that the beautiful child wrapped in His mother's arms would exit this world not with a crown of gold but of thorns, and not atop a king's chariot but on a cross of wood?

This Sunday, when you assemble in your local "house of bread," remember that His story is not just "history." You're part of it all. Christ the King is as alive and as close as you allow Him to be, even within you, changing you royally.

SALVATION GIVEN

But you, O Bethlehem,...
from you shall come forth for me
*   one who is to be ruler in Israel....*
He shall stand and feed his flock in the strength of the LORD,

in the majesty of the name of the LORD his God.
And they shall dwell secure, for now he shall be great
to the ends of the earth.

Micah 5:2–4

But in this world of sin,
where meek souls will receive Him still
the dear Christ enters in.[1]
And thank God He does.

If it's supposed to be a "Silent Night," why all this music?

Now therefore write this song, and teach it to the sons of Israel; put it in their mouths, that this song may be a witness for me.

Deuteronomy 31:19

SITUATION EXPLAINED

Are you the kind of person who loves to sing Christmas songs? Or do you just pretend to know the words and mouth them, like I do?

SOLUTION OFFERED

Before any signs of Thanksgiving are seen, smelled or heard—before the pie is made, before the first piece of turkey is served, even before the good china is brought out and the football schedule is eyed—there is another holiday gaining attention on the radio. We start hearing Christmas songs right after Halloween! It's too bad that there aren't more songs about Thanksgiving. (Thank you, Adam Sandler, for trying.)

And once Advent has begun, you'll hear Christmas hymns just about everywhere you go. It is the only time of year when lyrics usually reserved for churches make their way into the secular subconscious.

Maybe you love Christmas carols; maybe you've grown sick of them. In either case, given who most of the songs are about (and no, I'm not referring to Santa), they do deserve at least our respect.

So how do we help make sure that songs about God are received differently from the other holiday favorites? How do we follow the command set forth in the verse above? How do we ensure that when we hear the holy songs in homes or public settings they retain their prayerfulness and meaning?

Isn't it interesting that in today's society—where many people are trying hard to eliminate any and every trace of God, Jesus Christ, His Word and His church from every public building, school and holiday greeting—Christmas music is still accessible and even prevalent in public spaces? You can't stand in line at a Starbucks, walk through a mall or get put on hold without hearing about the fact that Jesus was born in a manger. Apparently you can hear about it while standing in a federal building, but you better not talk about it there.

There are literally thousands of Christmas carols that have been created, sung and echoed throughout the centuries. One of the most famous, "Silent Night," was first penned and performed in the early part of the nineteenth century. Accounts vary regarding the events surrounding its composition and often feature exaggerated tales spun to romanticize its beginnings. One need only look online to see a sampling of such stories, each outdoing the next. What we do know is that Father Joseph Mohr, a priest, wrote the words and then asked his friend, the musician Franz Gruber, to add a melody and guitar accompaniment. They performed their composition in a small Catholic church in Oberndorf, a tiny Austrian village, sometime around 1818.

The hymn must have struck a chord (ooh, that's a good pun) with Karl Mauracher, an organ builder and repairman from the area. Mauracher was so taken by the hymn that after he traveled to the church in Oberndorf, he asked for a copy of the composition and later shared it as he journeyed from place to place, fixing organs. For him it was more than a song; it was a prayer, an expression of praise offered for a living God who deserved to be praised. While the song was "silent," it left an impression in his heart that was anything but.[2]

Sometimes during the Advent season I find myself focusing more on the notes of Christmas songs than on the music, more on the words than on their meaning. Sometimes I fall into the trap of "singing a song about Jesus" instead of praying a song in my worship of Jesus. This is a little difference that can make a big difference.

The next time you hear one of those Christmas carols in church or even in a department store, focus on the prayer wrapped in the melody. Look around you and offer a prayer for all those you see—both those you know and those you don't know. You might share eternity with these people someday. Pray that they will allow the Lord into their lives, homes and holidays.

And if you're brave enough, sing a little. If people ask you why you're singing, take a step out in faith and tell them why. Tell them that God loved you enough to become nothing so that you could have everything. Tell them that He looks past your unworthiness and sees worth. That's what it means to pray a song, for every song about God (as this verse reminds us) should act as a witness of His greatness, His mercy and His love.

A humble priest, an organist and an organ repairman in a tiny town forever changed our Christmas celebrations. Imagine what one unknown but willing Christian from a little suburban neighborhood can do two hundred years later, given the courage to pray a song.

SALVATION GIVEN

Now therefore write this song, and teach it to the sons of Israel; put it in their mouths, that this song may be a witness for me.

Deuteronomy 31:19

Tonight might be a "silent night" in your world, but it doesn't have to be. Proclaim that Jesus Christ is not just your Lord but the Lord of all.

Have you untangled your Christmas lights yet?

So we, though many, are one body in Christ, and individually members one of another.

Romans 12:5

SITUATION EXPLAINED

Are you "into the season"?

SOLUTION OFFERED

Every winter across America, normal suburban neighborhoods are transformed into miniature versions of the Las Vegas strip. People all along the block, young and old alike, break out the stepladders and knotted strands of lights to signal that the Christmas season is in full swing.

Each year I partake in the yuletide tradition of decking my home with lights. Two years ago, in a hurry (as I usually am), I neglected to actually plug in and test any of the strands of lights I was putting up. I figured, "They were all working last year when I pulled them down, so why bother?"

Well, needless to say, when I finally plugged in my personal light show, it was less than spectacular. The random lights that did work made my house look more like a two-bit motel than the "Griswold home" that I was envisioning (for all you *Christmas Vacation* fans).

Why is it that if *one* bulb is burnt out, the rest of the strand doesn't work? Each bulb, although it has its own filament, depends on the bulbs around it and on the power that is fed to it.

Hmmm, kind of sounds like our community of faith. While our faith may not depend on other people, God has not designed us to "walk alone." The faith, our faith, is meant to be shared.

The verse above reminds us that, although at times we act only as one light in this world, all of us who consider ourselves Christian are bound together in a common strand. Of course, when you and I get "burnt out" or "tangled," God doesn't throw us out. We can look at the lights around us, see how brightly they're shining and realize that we need to change.

Those who "shine" around us are gifts from God. They offer an invitation to us to change our "bulb."

To all of you who have shown me that my bulb was looking dim, I say, "Thank you." I'm going to shine brighter this season because of you.

SALVATION GIVEN

So we, though many, are one body in Christ, and individually members one of another.

Romans 12:5

Remember, God's light strand is perfectly straight; we're the ones who get it all tangled.

Is your Christmas tree alive or dead?

For each tree is known by its own fruit.

Luke 6:44

SITUATION EXPLAINED

Is your tree bearing good fruit?

SOLUTION OFFERED

I bought my Christmas tree too early last year. Usually I hold off on getting one until the week before, so that I can enjoy the smell of a freshly cut tree for a couple weeks after Christmas. Last year, however, I got a little overexcited and purchased my tree about a week after Thanksgiving.

The day after Christmas I had to peel the lights from the brittle needles. I swept them up and carried the large, dry fire hazard out to the trash. I want to thank God for the inventor of the dustpan.

It saddened me a little bit. The tree was dead. The lights were down. Gifts needed to be returned. People started back to work and school. Christmas was over.

"What has changed in my life?" I asked myself. Beyond personal debt and the presents I received, "What was different?" I wondered.

Everything was different, actually, and not just for me.

If you open your heart even the slightest bit during the holiday season, then Jesus will become more present within you than before. If you love family and friends in even the smallest ways, Christ's love is made more visible. If you make it a point to brave the crowds not at the malls but at the churches, you give God yet another shot at you and receive His grace in a special way.

Like a real Christmas tree, over time I sometimes get spiritually dry; I may even feel as if I'm falling apart. Like an artificial Christmas tree, I might look great on the outside but my life is fake.

Some traditions have it that the tree became a popular symbol at Christmastime because of an eighth-century saint. Saint Boniface was a missionary who brought Christianity to Germany way back in the seven hundreds. Most of the Germans were worshiping false gods at the time, and some were even sacrificing humans. Saint Boniface cut down a giant oak tree (sacred to the patron god) and taught that it was a symbol of Christ: a sign of peace and of life.

Today's Christmas tree *points* to Christ, home in the heavens, waiting for us and calling us to join Him. And we use an evergreen to remind us that He is everlasting, and so is His love.

It hit me last Christmas that my tree is neither dead nor fake, and neither is yours. You and I *are* the Christmas tree. We are the symbols of Christ's love and light and life in this world. We are the ones who point up to Christ and take attention off the false gods that can blind our loved ones. We are real, living and breathing, even when we feel dried out, fake or even dead. We are living because Christ lives within us by virtue of our baptism.

May your legs, like a trunk, stand firm in the truth this year.

May your arms, like branches, uphold all of God's creation.

May your holiness, like the tree's scent, draw others closer to the Lord.

May your joy, like the lights, make others smile.

May your life, like the treetop, point directly to heaven.

Christ died on a tree so that we might live like one.

Salvation Given

For each tree is known by its own fruit.

Luke 6:44

May your tree stand tall in your homes, jobs and schools this entire year.

Ever wonder where Santa Claus came from?

Give ear, O my people, to my teaching;
incline your ears to the words of my mouth!
I will open my mouth in a parable;
I will utter dark sayings from of old,
things that we have heard and known,
that our fathers have told us.
We will not hide them from their children,
but tell to the coming generation
the glorious deeds of the LORD, and his might,
and the wonders which he has wrought.

Psalm 78:1–4

SITUATION EXPLAINED

Do you love a good story? I find that the true ones are the best.

SOLUTION OFFERED

OK, it's Advent, so let's sit back and review.

God, the Creator of all creation, became man. Moreover, He became a needy, delicate, vulnerable baby. And not only was He a baby but a baby born to poor, lower-middle-class parents. And as if that weren't enough, He wasn't even given a room or a home or a bed.

Seem too much to believe? Do you have a hard time putting your faith in such a figure?

For some folks the simple facts surrounding the birth of Jesus are just too much to comprehend, much less meditate on in prayer. Others feel that the truth of what God did by becoming man is a story that isn't sensational enough. How that is I'm not sure, because the Christmas story has all the beauty, intrigue and heroism we could want.

That being said, accepting it still requires faith and an open heart. Some people get more caught up with a star in the sky than the one in the manger. Many would rather read their futures in the stars than in heaven itself.

It's interesting that so many people in our culture can put their "faith" in Santa Claus but consider the story of Jesus to be a fabrication. Many of them don't realize that the Santa story is an extension and exaggeration of a great follower of Christ, Saint Nicholas.

Nicholas was born in what is now Turkey in AD 280, and he died on December 6, 343. He led a difficult life, beginning with being orphaned at the age of nine. He went on to study philosophy and Christian doctrine (no, not toy engineering) and was considered quite an outspoken troublemaker by Emperor Diocletian, who wanted him to stop preaching. Nicholas was jailed not once but twice for evangelizing. He was named a bishop of the church early in the fourth century.

Nicholas was known for his generosity. As tradition goes, he snuck up to his neighbor's house at night and dropped a handful of gold coins through the open window so that the eldest daughter could afford to get married. He repeated the generous act for the two younger daughters. From there the Santa legend grew into what we mark today with stockings, chimneys, a belly like jelly and all that good stuff. [3]

The true life story of Saint Nicholas is one of suffering, simplicity, generosity and humility. The nativity of Jesus is the same kind of story. Neither story was "seen by millions," but both are true. Both stories have changed our modern world, and one of them opened the gates of heaven.

Make no mistake, both stories have happy endings, one with gifts under a tree and the other with the gift of salvation who hung from a tree and rose again. He is Jesus, your Lord and Savior. He is God, and He came down here for you. Saint Nicholas, while a holy man, was still just a man. And Santa's magic, though it might warm the heart of a scrooge, cannot turn a heart to God or save a soul.

Our ancestors, our brothers and sisters in the faith, knew the power of a good story. As we see in this passage from Psalms, they took seriously their need to pass along stories not for the sake of entertainment but for the truths of faith in the stories. To do so was to follow the commands of God; not to do so was to muffle God's voice to a young generation in need of it.

SALVATION GIVEN

Give ear, O my people, to my teaching;
*   incline your ears to the words of my mouth!*
I will open my mouth in a parable;
*   I will utter dark sayings from of old,*
things that we have heard and known,
*   that our fathers have told us.*
We will not hide them from their children,
*   but tell to the coming generation*
the glorious deeds of the LORD, and his might,
*   and the wonders which he has wrought.*

Psalm 78:1–4

'Twas just weeks before Christmas
and all through the church,
many hearts were stirring
but still evading God's search.

Were you ever afraid of Santa?

The eyes of the LORD are in every place,
keeping watch on the evil and the good.

Proverbs 15:3

SITUATION EXPLAINED

Are you ready for Santa? More importantly, are you ready for Jesus?

SOLUTION OFFERED

Stop and count. How many days until Santa Claus arrives?

As a child, was there any sunrise that you looked forward to more than the one on Christmas morning? The anticipation, the wonderment and the excitement of Christmas are enough to coax millions of children into better behavior 364 days a year. Santa Claus is watching.

I vividly recall my mother's reminder that Santa knew "if we had been bad or good,...for goodness' sake." And while my parents raised me in an educated and loving Catholic household, I had a far healthier fear of upsetting Santa Claus than of letting down God. Disappointing Jesus carried consequences that my young mind could not fathom, but disappoint the big boy in red and I'd be playin' with a lump of coal for the next year.

Incidentally, for those optimists out there who think that coal is better than nothing, you're wrong. Coal stinks. It's not even fun accidentally.

Truthfully, fear of Santa kept me in line on hundreds of occasions. Isn't it interesting that the threat of lost presents can make a child behave better? Why is it that the possible loss of toys or other material possessions can turn a brat into an angel?

That being said, why is it that the awe of God doesn't keep this adult in line? Why doesn't the reality of sin and its consequences motivate me to love God more deeply and more urgently on a daily basis? Why don't I fight harder against behavior that makes it more difficult for me to experience God's fullness? Why don't I have enough awe and love for my Creator to silence me in my anger, humble me in my pride, awaken me in my shortsightedness and rattle me out of my complacency? What "gift" of this world is so worthy that I let it dominate my attention? How could I ever let something temporary or passing (like momentary happiness or material goods) take my focus off the everlasting life of God in heaven?

I think that for a lot of Christians, many days are spent in sort of a "don't make God angry" type of mindset. That was my mindset for a better portion of my life. I lived to "keep God happy with me" and remain on His good side—kind of like my approach to Santa while growing up.

I used to tell people that Santa Claus was a felon. Since I didn't give him permission to come into the house, he was guilty of breaking and entering. Jesus doesn't work that way. If you want Christ to enter you fully, you need to ask. God respects your free will; after all, He gave it to you.

No, Jesus won't "break and enter," but He will "enter and break." Once He is in, you will be even more broken than when you invited Him. And that brokenness is a good thing; in fact, it's a great thing. In your brokenness Christ can work. In your brokenness you can experience who He is: your Savior, the only one who can heal your wounds, make sense of your life and get you to heaven.

Today, wake up with wide-eyed enthusiasm. Go beyond merely "keeping God happy" to a deeper relationship with God than the one you had yesterday.

Jesus sees you when you're sleeping.

Christ knows when you're awake.

God knows when you've been bad or good,

so be *great* for goodness' sake.[4]

SALVATION GIVEN

The eyes of the LORD are in every place,

keeping watch on the evil and the good.

Proverbs 15:3

Don't freak at the small number of shopping days before Christmas. Take courage and hit the mall. (I wear a large, by the way.)

Do you like to open gifts early?

Therefore, beloved, since you wait for these, be zealous to be found by him without spot or blemish, and at peace. And count the forbearance of our Lord as salvation....There are some things in them hard to understand, which the ignorant and unstable twist to their own destruction, as they do the other Scriptures. You therefore, beloved, knowing this beforehand, beware lest you be carried away with the error of lawless men and lose your own stability. But grow in the grace and knowledge of our Lord and Savior Jesus Christ.

2 Peter 3:14–18

SITUATION EXPLAINED

Patience is a virtue, they say. Do you want it right now?

SOLUTION OFFERED

Growing up, I really annoyed my mom at Christmastime. The minute the tree and lights went up, I began asking the question, and I asked it daily: "Can I open one of my Christmas presents early? Can I, Mom? Can I?"

The closer we got to Christmas Day, the more frequent and the louder the begging became. I was so impatient. I imagined the joy that the present would bring and didn't want to wait. I couldn't wait, even though I was the kid who two days after Christmas would be bored with the new toys and go back to his old standbys.

Some people carry this impatience into adulthood. "You only live once," they say. "Do whatever makes you feel good; God wants you to be happy." "If God didn't want us to have sex when we're teenagers, why would He create us with the urge?" some use for an excuse.

A friend once told me that God wanted him to smoke weed. "God created it for that purpose. He wants me to smoke it because it makes me happy." With total love I said, "You're listening to the *wrong* burning bush, Bro."

This "do whatever makes you feel good because God wants us to be happy" idea is a popular statement in today's culture. The problem is that it is totally backward. God wants us to be more than happy; He wants us to be joyful. He wants us to have life.

Happiness is a feeling that passes; joy is a decision, the conviction to keep our focus on Christ and on heaven, no matter what is happening in our day. True joy comes from knowing God, believing in His plan for you and trusting in His love and in His promise of heaven for you.

"Do whatever makes you feel good" is, in all honesty, terrible advice. It leads to loneliness, addiction and death. It is rooted in the temporary things of this world rather than in the forever. It's passing and shallow. In short, it's rooted in selfishness.

Really, the Christmas season, like life, is all about patience and trust. That is what this verse is telling us. God wants joy for us even more than we do, because He knows that true joy is heaven. Joy doesn't come from doing what makes you happy; happiness comes from being who you are designed to be, and we only learn that by knowing the Designer.

God has a plan for you that only you can fulfill. You can run from it or run toward it, but in the long run that is life, which will bring you more joy?

SALVATION GIVEN

Therefore, beloved, since you wait for these, be zealous to be found by him without spot or blemish, and at peace. And count the forbear-

ance of our Lord as salvation....There are some things in them hard to understand, which the ignorant and unstable twist to their own destruction, as they do the other Scriptures. You therefore, beloved, knowing this beforehand, beware lest you be carried away with the error of lawless men and lose your own stability. But grow in the grace and knowledge of our Lord and Savior Jesus Christ.

2 Peter 3:14–18

God's present is His presence, and He's always worth the wait.

Chapter Three

Encountering God During Lent and Easter

Discovering the yoke in the Easter egg

What's the deal with Lent?

Do not neglect to do good and to share what you have, for such sacrifices are pleasing to God.

Hebrews 13:16

SITUATION EXPLAINED

What are you giving up for Lent? Why?

SOLUTION OFFERED

When I was a kid, Lent didn't mean a whole lot. It meant getting a filet-o-fish instead of a cheeseburger in my usual Friday Happy Meal. It meant that the music at Mass got more serious, and we didn't say the "A" word: you know, Allelu———.

It also meant that Easter was coming soon. And you know what that meant? An Easter egg hunt against my brothers!

It seems that many Catholics who "give things up" for Lent don't really know why. Often they proceed to make the rest of the world miserable. An example: I tried giving up caffeine one year. Not a good idea. It took a couple weeks for the headaches to wear off, but even after that I was still pretty difficult to get along with. OK, I was impossible to get along with.

So what really is the big deal with Lent, and what's the point of those sacrifices anyway?

The word *Lent* comes from the Anglo-Saxon *lencten*, which basically means "spring." Why spring, you ask?

Well, because spring is about life. The trees and flowers come back to life in spring, and life is what Easter is about. The death of Good Friday and the *life* of Easter Sunday—that's what we call the Paschal Mystery.

And in order to rise like Jesus, we must first die. Lent is the church's "spiritual wake-up call" to prepare us for Easter and to remind us that we need to die to ourselves. Dying to yourself means dying to your own wants, pleasures, desires and so on in order to focus on what God wants for you in your life. Lent is a great time to reprioritize.

When we sacrifice anything during Lent, either something we "need" (caffeine) or something we enjoy (candy), it's the sacrifice that counts. The sacrifice isn't meant to make us miserable but to help us keep in mind the much greater sacrifice God made for us on the cross.

SALVATION GIVEN

Do not neglect to do good and to share what you have, for such sacrifices are pleasing to God.

Hebrews 13:16

Sacrifice without a little discomfort is probably not a sacrifice.

Why do we get ashes on our foreheads?

Then I turned my face to the Lord God, seeking him by prayer and supplications with fasting and sackcloth and ashes. I prayed to the LORD my God and made confession, saying, "O Lord, the great and awesome God,...we have sinned and done wrong and acted wickedly and rebelled, turning aside from your commandments and ordinances; we have not listened to your servants."

Daniel 9:3–6

SITUATION EXPLAINED

Is there a purpose to running around with a dirty forehead on Ash Wednesday?

SOLUTION OFFERED

"Excuse me, you've got some dirt on your head."

Every year someone says that to me on Ash Wednesday. Maybe it has happened to you too. In the past it used to frustrate me, but in recent years I have come to see it as a great opportunity to evangelize, to share with someone about the most important person in my life: Jesus Christ.

So what do you say when folks ask you about that smudge?

Here are a few responses that I would *not* recommend:

The Ignorant Response: "My mom made me go to church and get them. I have no idea what they mean."

The Sarcastic Response: "I'm protesting showers. Today, ashes; tomorrow I'm going to swim in raw sewage."

The Ridiculous Response: "I have a big zit that I'm trying to cover up. Is it working?"

The Practical (but Misguided) Response: "Better dirty on the outside of my head than on the inside."

And here are a few responses that I *would* recommend:

The Biblical Response: Over forty passages in the Bible associate ashes with mourning and grief. In Old Testament times people used ashes as a sign of repentance. They would sit in ashes, roll around in them, sprinkle them on their heads or even mingle them with their food and drink. They did this as an outward sign of their inward posture of repentance.

Ash Wednesday begins Lent, a time when we stop and assess how we're doing in our walk with God. Lent helps us identify spiritual areas in which we can grow and sinful areas that we need to avoid. To repent, put simply, means to turn *away* from sin and turn *toward* God. We use ashes as an outward expression of our need to begin again.

A Traditional Response: Ashes are a sign of physical death, as in "ashes to ashes, dust to dust." We began as dust (a joyless and lifeless existence), and our bodies will return to dust until we are raised up by Christ. By receiving ashes and keeping them on, we publicly proclaim our intent to die to our worldly desires and live even more in Christ's image, which we focus on during the season of rebirth that is Lent.

The Historical Response: For over twelve hundred years, on the *dies cinerum* (day of ashes) faithful followers have approached the altar and received ashes on their foreheads. These ashes are made from the burnt palm fronds that were blessed on the Palm Sunday of the previous year. The ashes are sprinkled with holy water, usually fragranced with incense and blessed using four prayers that are thousands of years old.

The use of ashes for repentance and penance can be traced even further back and is practiced throughout the world. On Ash Wednesday ashes are applied to believers' foreheads in the shape of the cross.

The Symbolic Response: God formed Adam out of the "dust" of the earth, which we read about in Genesis 2:7. In addition, Jesus healed the blind man with clay (earth and spit) in John 9:6. We mark ourselves with ashes as a "new beginning" at the onset of Lent, allowing the life of Jesus Christ to make us whole and new again.

The Most Basic Response: I'm a sinner. I don't always love God as strongly as I could or as directly as I should. Ash Wednesday reminds me that it is only through God that I have life; He gave it to me.

Ash Wednesday also begins my preparation for Holy Week and the Passion and Resurrection of my Lord Jesus, without whom I have no life here and no chance at eternal life in heaven. This is just a great opportunity for me to get better.

Thanks for asking.

SALVATION GIVEN

Then I turned my face to the Lord God, seeking him by prayer and supplications with fasting and sackcloth and ashes. I prayed to the LORD my God and made confession, saying, "O Lord, the great and awesome God,…we have sinned and done wrong and acted wickedly and rebelled, turning aside from your commandments and ordinances; we have not listened to your servants.

Daniel 9:3–6

God forgives, He loves, and He gives this sinner a second chance. Put simply: My God kicks ash.

What's the purpose of abstinence?

So you also must consider yourselves dead to sin and alive to God in Christ Jesus. Let not sin therefore reign in your mortal bodies, to make you obey their passions....For just as you once yielded your members to impurity and to greater and greater iniquity, so now yield your members to righteousness.

Romans 6:11–12, 19

SITUATION EXPLAINED

What factors guide your decisions in the course of the day?

SOLUTION OFFERED

Before I was married someone once asked me, "Do you practice *abstinence* on Fridays during Lent?"

"I'm single. I practice abstinence and chastity every day," I replied.

While I was being honest, the person didn't get my joke. Incidentally, I know that it wasn't that funny, but it still made me laugh, which is not difficult to do.

The person asking was inquiring as to whether or not I abstained from eating meat on Fridays during the Lenten season, which I do. It did get me thinking, however, about the word *abstinence* and its bigger meaning in my life.

Abstinence from meat is more than "going without" or a reminder of the fact that Christ offered His flesh for us on the cross. Abstinence is a form of prayer, a discipline. When we abstain from meat, we focus on Christ and on our souls, rather than on self and on our bodies. It is faith in action, placing our attention on Jesus and offering Him "our flesh" as a sacrifice (see Romans 12:1–2), a vessel through which He can and does work.

Abstinence from meat, from drugs, from alcohol, from

premarital sex—really, from anything that might, can or does take our attention away from God—is a wonderful blessing. It is an example of how we can make our flesh slaves to our souls. That is what Saint Paul is talking about in this verse from Romans.

A single person continually choosing to live in chastity, "abstaining" from premarital sex, is a beautiful example of a soul driving flesh and not vice versa. Likewise, even simpler gestures of going without—such as abstaining from meat on a Friday—are great instances of sacrifice. God rewards such offerings with immeasurable grace.

When you can't have something is obviously when it becomes all the more appealing. That problem began in the Garden of Eden. Sex is appealing to unmarrieds; snacking between meals seems more desirable when you're fasting; abstaining from meat might seem almost impossible when you're "forced" to do it.

Those moments of temptation don't have to lead to frustration, though. Not if we are aware. Not if we pray. Not if we refuse, in those moments, to allow our bodies and minds to dictate the actions of our souls.

God has given us our souls, and He designed them to praise and bless. He also fills our souls with power. Though body and soul are intertwined intimately and completely, that doesn't mean that one can't "take the lead." Your soul *can* control your body. Pray for this.

Use times like Lent to recognize areas in your life where your body leads your soul into dangerous waters. Identify them, ask God for help, and eliminate them.

Next, remember the acronym "BATHS." It stands for "bored, angry, tired, hungry and stressed." If you are any of the five, be aware that you are more vulnerable to temptation. Don't allow yourself to become a slave to your emotions.

Jesus experienced the same types of emotions that you do daily. When faced with those emotions (like in the Garden of Gethsemane), He prayed. That is faith in action.

Lent is a spiritual workout. It is a gift. Don't abstain from the discipline and grace that await you during this time. Don't let a moment of weakness dictate your future. Don't let a mistake become a tradition. When you fall, admit it, reconcile and move on.

Every *body* might not have rhythm, but thanks to God, we all have *soul.*

SALVATION GIVEN

So you also must consider yourselves dead to sin and alive to God in Christ Jesus. Let not sin therefore reign in your mortal bodies, to make you obey their passions....For just as you once yielded your members to impurity and to greater and greater iniquity, so now yield your members to righteousness.

Romans 6:11–12, 19

Jesus carrying the cross: there is an example of a soul driving the body.

Why do we abstain from *meat* during Lent?

Since therefore Christ suffered in the flesh, arm yourselves with the same thought, for whoever has suffered in the flesh has ceased from sin.

1 Peter 4:1

SITUATION EXPLAINED

Skip the burgers (unless they're veggie) on Fridays during Lent.

SOLUTION OFFERED

Picture it: You're in a hurry. You're focused on school or work or family or friends, where there are a thousand things going on. You stop "real quick" to eat in the middle of the day. Halfway through the meal—or a little while after—you remember it's Friday. And it's Lent! And that's a burger in your stomach!!

In the words of Homer Simpson, "D'oh!"

This has happened to me before, and odds are that it has happened at one time or another to you. A side note here to anyone who may be worrying or feeling guilty right now: If you forget, then no, it is not a sin.

We've discussed abstinence and its purpose in our spiritual lives, but why do we abstain from *meat*?

Actually, people offer several reasons for why the church embraces this discipline, a tradition that dates back hundreds of years. Some say it was because the church was trying to support the fishing industry when times were tough. The church was trying to keep fishermen "afloat" (yes, pun intended). There is some historical evidence of that, dating all the way back to the second century.

Some say it was safer to eat fish than meat. Everyone knew the specific time frame in which it was safe to eat fish, while people tended to test the time frame with beef. There's some historical evidence for that too, dating back to about the seventh century.

Some point out that hundreds of years ago only the very wealthy could afford meat. Fish (in comparison) was the poor man's meal. It was cheap, humble food that you had to catch yourself.

Some say that not eating meat helped folks to focus on the humility of Christ, who lived a simple man's life. Others tie in symbolic significance: We should eat fish instead of meat to remind us that we are "little fish" of the "great fish," Jesus Christ.

There are literally dozens of other explanations for this discipline's evolution over the years and the church's maintenance of it. They are good to know, but they didn't help me a lot when I was a teenager. I just knew that I wanted meat.

If we aren't focusing on Jesus and on the cross when we abstain from meat, then the matter can become less about Lent and more about "should I have the meatless pizza or the grilled cheese sandwich?" We all know that it's so much more than that.

I prefer to look at it like this: Jesus Christ, my Lord and my Savior, gave up His own body, *His own flesh,* that Friday so many years ago, for me and for you. He went through the pain of that self-sacrifice, completely mindful of God the Father. When I go through the incredibly minor act of abstaining from meat on Fridays, it is just one tiny act of self-sacrifice that points me back to that awful but Good Friday. That was the Friday when God loved me so much that He gave up His flesh in the most selfless act in history.

Thinking about how often my physical body can lead me into sin and away from God, it is great to have a chance to let my body help lead me out of sin and toward God. That's the essence of this verse below. Pray it again.

SALVATION GIVEN

Since therefore Christ suffered in the flesh, arm yourselves with the same thought, for whoever has suffered in the flesh has ceased from sin.

1 Peter 4:1

Meat is great, but Jesus seemed to do pretty well with just bread and fish, and so did everyone else who received the multiplied food (see Matthew 15:34–37).

Why do you love Jesus?

For I received from the Lord what I also delivered to you, that the Lord Jesus on the night when he was betrayed took bread, and when he had given thanks, he broke it, and said, "This is my body which is for you. Do this in remembrance of me."

1 Corinthians 11:23–24

SITUATION EXPLAINED

Do you love Jesus for who He is or for what He does?

SOLUTION OFFERED

It is easy to get caught up in praising and thanking God for the things that He does. That is good; don't get me wrong. The thing is, however, that God wants us to love Him for *who He is* (our Father) beyond just loving Him for what He does (save us).

What adjectives do you use to describe the Lord Jesus? I scribbled a few:

> Everlasting, eternal
> Unlimited, unconditional, universal
> Courageous, compassionate
> Humble, holy
> All-powerful, all-loving, all-knowing
> Relentless, reckless, revolutionary
> Indefinable, inspiring, intriguing
> Sacred, spiritual, soul-loving
> Trustworthy, triumphant

The words across are just a handful of the adjectives that I use to describe my God.

The word down is the noun in which I come to know Him more personally and more deeply *in the flesh* and for real: EUCHARIST. It is spelled down, just as Jesus, the Living Bread, came down from heaven.

While Jesus in the flesh is beyond description, beyond these words, He still comprises all of them.

- Through the Eucharist Jesus' physical love is everlasting, and His presence is eternally among us.
- Through the Eucharist we experience His unlimited mercy, unconditional love and universal (Catholic) call to community at the table.
- In the Eucharist we see His courage and compassion in giving Himself totally, and we are called to be more courageous preachers of truth and more compassionate brothers and sisters.
- Through the Eucharist we are made more humble and strive to be holier.
- Through the Eucharist the all-powerful, all-loving, all-knowing Creator and God comes to us as *Abba,* Father, adopting us as His own "flesh and blood."
- Through the Eucharist Jesus is relentless in blessing us, reckless in His love and revolutionary in His work in our hearts.
- Through the Eucharist the indefinable is experienced, the hopeless are inspired and the ambivalent are intrigued.
- Through the Eucharist we live the sacred life of the Spirit, and our souls are filled and nourished.
- Through the Eucharist our trust in eternal salvation is confirmed, and the Lamb is triumphant in our lives.

Jesus took the bread and the cup and *gave thanks* (see Matthew 26:26–27). As you may or may not know, the word

Eucharist is the Greek word for "thanksgiving." As the church teaches and the Scriptures affirm, it is more than a simple meal for giving thanks; it is Christ giving Himself to us, in the forever sacrifice, the eternal blessing.

Indeed, Christ accomplishes much through the Eucharist, but that is not why we adore Him. For we do not adore things *about* Jesus; we adore Jesus Christ, true God, in the flesh.

Make no mistake, that is what Saint Paul taught, and he was not even in the Upper Room that night. The apostles handed on this truth of the Eucharist to Saint Paul years later, and he believed it with his whole heart, as we see in these verses today.

The next time you're looking for God, look no further than the altar. He is there, ready and waiting for you.

Salvation Given

For I received from the Lord what I also delivered to you, that the Lord Jesus on the night when he was betrayed took bread, and when he had given thanks, he broke it, and said, "This is my body which is for you. Do this in remembrance of me."

1 Corinthians 11:23–24

Today give thanks to the Lord for who He is, not solely for what He does.

What is the greatest achievement of your life?

From now on there is laid up for me the crown of righteousness, which the Lord, the righteous judge, will award to me on that Day, and not only to me but also to all who have loved his appearing.

2 Timothy 4:8

SITUATION EXPLAINED

The crowning moment of your life is yet to come.

SOLUTION OFFERED

What do you consider the highlight of your life? Maybe you hit the winning shot, got the solo in the recital, were elected to student council or made homecoming court. Maybe you got the grade up in your worst subject, worked up the courage to ask out that one person you really liked, had an article published in the newspaper or were nominated for an award. Possibly you graduated, served in the military, started your own business or got the big promotion. Maybe you came into the church at Easter. Maybe you were married or even ordained.

Whether others considered the moment "big" or "small" is not as important as how you were touched and blessed by it and how you glorified God through it. Yet more important is to recognize that, no matter how great your moment was, it was not *the* crowning moment of your life. That is yet to come.

There were many great moments in Jesus' ministry. He preached to thousands, changed the water into wine at Cana, cleansed the temple, healed all sorts of illnesses, even raised the dead. But none of these was Jesus' crowning achievement.

Jesus received a crown from the soldiers who mocked Him; it was a crown of thorns that dug into His scalp (see Matthew 27:29). That was one more crowning moment in His life, a time when He demonstrated His godliness, His manhood and His love, through mercy and peace.

But the crowning achievement of Jesus' life came after His death, when He rose from the dead and walked out of that tomb. It was at that moment that all the previous moments were glorified and magnified, pointing back to the heavenly Father.

Like most artists, it took death for Jesus' life to be understood. (Of course, Jesus was more than "another artist": His life brings life; it doesn't just represent it the way artists do.) The Resurrection proved Him to be more than a preacher, teacher, healer or political leader. The Resurrection proved that He is God.

You might go on to accomplish great things with your life. You might become a famous musician, an accomplished actor, a life-changing parent, a respected physician, a renowned designer, a servant priest or religious, an amazing athlete, a popular author, an inspirational speaker, a motivating teacher, an honorable soldier, or you might pursue any one of hundreds of other vocations that will glorify God. The truth, though, is that as successful as you may or may not become by the world's standards, and no matter how many crowning moments you may have in your life, these will be miniscule when compared to your resurrection.

Imagine having Jesus look you in the eyes and say, "My beloved child, well done. Come and see what I have prepared for you." That will be the crowning achievement of your life, a life designed to love and serve others.

Salvation Given

From now on there is laid up for me the crown of righteousness, which the Lord, the righteous judge, will award to me on that Day, and not only to me but also to all who have loved his appearing.

2 Timothy 4:8

Live a life that others will remember years from now, not because it points to you but because it points to the One who created you.

What's so good about Good Friday?

Come now, let us reason together,
*   says the LORD:*
though your sins are like scarlet,
*   they shall be as white as snow;*
though they are red like crimson,
*   they shall become like wool.*

Isaiah 1:18

SITUATION EXPLAINED

How can we see the cross as a good thing?

SOLUTION OFFERED

I am a sinner. How could God forgive me for all that I have done in my life? How can God forget about all of the times I've been selfish? How could my Creator possibly still love me, knowing all the things I've done?

How indeed? Only the cross "crosses" out all of that garbage.

The cross has been called glorious, magnificent and wonderful, but how can the cross of Jesus be such a good thing? The wonderful cross: what is it?

It is the eternal reminder that sin is death, but death has no power over me.

It is a challenge to my self-centeredness, forcing me to look beyond myself.

It is a harsh reality that necessitates a decision and action on my part as a Christian.

It is a sacrifice so steeped in love that I can barely comprehend it.

It is the sword my Savior wields to defend and uplift me.

It is the entryway to heaven, the doorway to a happiness that I can only imagine.

It is the invitation into the eternal family, to a seat at the banquet table of God my Father.

No, I'm not worthy, but worthiness has nothing to do with me and everything to do with God. That is how incredibly and realistically God loves you and me. He knows how sin clouds and clogs our relationships.

This verse reminds us of how badly our Father wants things to be made right and how easy it is if we go to Him. In our unworthiness He finds worth; in our sinfulness the cross stands firm, raising us up the way the Romans raised up my Savior on Good Friday. The verse also reminds us of the fact that God raised up our Lord one Sunday, an event we pause to remember each Sunday and every day we breathe.

I don't understand what God sees in me, but I am so glad that He does.

We've all sinned; we've all screwed up. If it's dragging you down, get to the sacrament of reconciliation right away. He is waiting. Are you walking? The only sin God cannot forgive is the sin for which we don't ask forgiveness.

SALVATION GIVEN
Come now, let us reason together,
*   says the LORD:*
* though your sins are like scarlet,*
*   they shall be as white as snow;*
* though they are red like crimson,*
*   they shall become like wool.*

Isaiah 1:18

You are worth more to God than you know, more than you can understand, for now; one day you will.

How could a loving God let His only Son die?

[Jesus] said to his disciples, "You know that after two days the Passover is coming, and the Son of man will be delivered up to be crucified."

Matthew 26:1–2

Situation Explained

It's hard to understand why God, who is all love, could allow His Son Jesus to die on the cross.

Solution Offered

The following story has been told and retold by people all over the world. It's told in different ways, but it communicates a beautiful reality.

Ever been across one of those bridges that goes up and down over rivers? You know, they go down for cars or trains to move across, but get put up to allow ships on the river to pass under. Nowadays they're all computerized, but years back people operated them.

One day a bridge operator heard an oncoming train signaling, but when he pressed the necessary buttons to lower the bridge, it didn't move. He tried again, and still nothing. He grew nervous, knowing that he would have to go outside the booth, crank the necessary gears, pull the lever and lower the bridge by hand. This was a difficult task. He would have to hold down the lever as hard as he could so as to be sure that the bridge was completely down.

The man ran out and did what he needed to do. He put every ounce of muscle he had into holding down the lever. Then, as he saw the train coming around the bend, he heard laughter. He looked up, and on the train tracks a little ways down, he saw his son, his only child, playing.

The father panicked, and his heart sank. His son was too far away to get to. He shouted repeatedly to him, but his son couldn't hear him. If he let go of the lever, the bridge would rise and the train would derail, killing thousands. If he held the lever down, his only son would die. He screamed with all his might, but it was no use.

With tears streaming down his cheeks, the father looked up to heaven. Then, bowing his head, he closed his eyes, clenched his teeth and held down the lever, sacrificing his only son to save the lives of many, most of whom would never know or understand the sacrifice that he made or how difficult it was.[1]

Was it easy for God to sacrifice his only Son? No, but that's how much He loves you. Love is all about sacrifice.

SALVATION GIVEN

[Jesus] said to his disciples, "You know that after two days the Passover is coming, and the Son of man will be delivered up to be crucified."

Matthew 26:1–2

Without Good Friday, Easter Sunday means nothing. Thank You, God.

What does it take to change your life?

And those who passed by derided him, wagging their heads.... And the robbers who were crucified with him also reviled him in the same way.

Matthew 27:39, 44

SITUATION EXPLAINED

Can your entire life change in one afternoon? What would God need to do for you to trust Him completely?

SOLUTION OFFERED

Sometimes going deeper in our faith just requires looking at things a little more closely. The verse above really struck me when I studied it again. I noticed that the noun *robbers* was plural, not singular.

Over the years I got so used to the fact that one of the criminals was "the good thief" and the other "the bad" that I missed (or forgot) the fact that when the actual crucifixion began on Golgotha, *both* the criminals were mocking our Lord. As the hours wore on under the darkening skies that afternoon, an often overlooked miracle took place in the midst of the torture: Even in the final hours, even in almost breathless agony, another sinner's heart turned to our Lord.

Why this transformation? Why the change in behavior? What was it that allowed this criminal's heart to open, his anger to subside and his attitude to change? What "clicked" inside of him?

Well, we know that the thieves were two of the people closest (in proximity) to Jesus, alongside the soldiers gambling for His clothes, the centurion, some of His persecutors, the women and a few others. It must have been mind-boggling for the thief to witness anyone so forgiving, so loving and so trusting in God at such a horrific and painful moment. It was that observance that offered the thief the confidence and humility to approach the Lord for forgiveness.

Have you ever had a personal experience with Christ like that, perhaps in His forgiveness of you? Do you remember it? Can you see Jesus *that* closely today? Many days I can't—or I should say, I don't.

How close are you to the cross? I know, it seems like a weird question at first, but have you thought about it? Have you meditated upon what happened on that hill that day? Have you ever closed your eyes, pictured God's face and seen Him look into your eyes? Have you heard Him call you by name? Can you hear Him inviting you to live forever?

Acknowledging Jesus for who He was took trust on the criminal's part, far more than it should take on my part. Why do I sometimes act as though Jesus won't respond to me with what I need? Pause and reflect.

Jesus is always quick to act. Think of the woman at the well, Peter in the sea, the Centurion's servant, Jairus's daughter, Peter's mother-in-law, the lepers, the blind man, the woman with the hemorrhage, the demoniacs, the woman caught in adultery, Lazarus in the grave, the high priest's servant in the garden. The list goes on and on and on.

Jesus goes beyond what we ask for. He is never outdone in generosity.

We said, "Forgive us," and He said, "I'll do even better, I'll adopt you" (see Galatians 4:4–5).

We said, "We're lowly," and He said, "The lowly will be exalted" (see Matthew 18:4; 20:27; 23:12).

We said, "How do we approach God?" and He said, "As *Abba,* Daddy" (see Mark 14:36; Romans 8:15; Galatians 4:6).

We said, "Teach us how to pray," and He gave us the Our Father (see Matthew 6:9–13).

We said, "We're hungry," and He fed us. He still does in the Eucharist (see John 6).

We said, "Show us how to live," and He said, "First you must die" (see John 12:24–25).

We said, "We don't want to die," and He opened the door to eternal life.

We said, "What is love?" and He mounted the cross.

The thief was not the only person touched or transformed by his proximity to Christ on the cross; others were that day and every single day since then for almost two thousand years.

This day look into His eyes, listen to His voice and experience how He loves. Be sure to watch closely.

SALVATION GIVEN

And those who passed by derided him, wagging their heads.... And the robbers who were crucified with him also reviled him in the same way.

Matthew 27:39, 44

Get close to the cross and close to Christ, the best place to be.

Jesus, the martial artist?

They will make war on the Lamb, and the Lamb will conquer them, for he is Lord of lords and King of kings, and those with him are called and chosen and faithful.

Revelation 17:14

SITUATION EXPLAINED

How did Jesus beat the devil? I mean, he died a terrible death on the cross. Didn't that make the devil happy?

SOLUTION OFFERED

No offense to Jackie Chan or Jet Li, but God is the ultimate martial artist. That's right, Jesus knows judo.

In the art of judo you learn many things, one of which is how to use your opponents' strengths against them. When done correctly, even a small person can render a much larger, stronger opponent completely powerless.

The devil's greatest strength is death. The devil's ultimate goal is death: to kill us. He loved every minute of Good Friday more than the last, as they cursed our King, beat Him, spit on Him, mocked Him and finally nailed Him to the cross. The devil thought he had won as Jesus hung there loving us with His blood.

Yet as the afternoon wore on, Christ stared death in the eye. And on Easter God showed us just how powerful and wise He really is.

As the master of "spiritual judo," God uses the devil's greatest strength (death) against him. Through Christ's blood we are not damned by death but saved by it. Christ's blood type turns a negative into a positive for all believers.

In the shadow of the cross, death is destroyed. That weak little Lamb beat back the powerful beast. The story of Christ is the story of a warrior, and His story changed our history, yours and mine, forever.

SALVATION GIVEN

They will make war on the Lamb, and the Lamb will conquer them, for he is Lord of lords and King of kings, and those with him are called and chosen and faithful.

Revelation 17:14

Who knew that Jesus was so tough? Anyone who reads His book knows.

Do you believe in love at first sight?

Charm is deceitful, and beauty is vain.

Proverbs 31:30

SITUATION EXPLAINED

Things are not always as they appear. Love looks beyond what we see.

SOLUTION OFFERED

An elderly couple recounted the details of their first date. The wife offered an incredibly detailed account of the night that the two met at a dance, including what her groom-to-be was wearing, the song the band played during their first dance, the name of the waiter they tipped to get a romantic table, what they both ordered to eat and so on. The night they had met some fifty years earlier was fresh in her memory.

Following the heartfelt sharing of his bride, the husband smiled, gazed into her eyes and said, "I have to be honest, Sweetheart. When I asked you to dance, I was speaking to your friend standing next to you. When you agreed, I felt so awkward that I went along with it."

The wife was speechless.

"But," the husband continued, "that mistake was the greatest thing that ever happened to me. It changed my life forever and for the better. I didn't see what or who was right in front of me, but now I realize that all along you were God's plan for me. I'm the luckiest, happiest man on Earth, and I love you more now than on the day I caught first sight of you."

The wife's eyes welled with tears, and they rose out of their chairs, took one another's hands and moved their frail bodies slowly across the floor. Their hearts beat with a renewed love.

Sometimes love at first sight is not exactly that. In fact, love at first sight seems like a fairy-tale notion to most people these days.

People handle dating and courtship in various ways. Sure, the romantics out there want the Cinderella story: everything beautiful, no sadness. The more practical folks want a partner who makes sense and is "perfect on paper." Those afraid of getting hurt (again) remain at a distance and risk never knowing true love. Those who think they lack anything to offer in a relationship sit alone and wonder. Still others try to control love, allowing people to see only what they want them to. Others engage in a battle between who they are and who they want to be.

And then there are the courageous ones, the ones who jump right in and say, "This is who I am. I'm not perfect. Can you love me?" They're fun and they're often fulfilled.

These relationship examples are not relevant just for romantic encounters but for our relationship to Christ as well. To be honest, when most people first encounter the gospel message, it is not a "love at first sight" kind of experience. If it is proclaimed truthfully, the gospel is challenging, unsettling and demanding. It is frightening yet calming, appalling yet affirming and complex yet simple. It causes us to reevaluate not only our perceptions of God but also our perceptions of ourselves.

The image of Jesus that you had when you were growing up and listening to Bible stories is not the image you get reading the Bible as a grown-up. The encounters are confrontational, the truths are stark, and the messages demand responses. The Crucifixion is the greatest example of such a reality. If you believe in love at first sight, the Crucifixion of our Lord makes you *take a second look*.

"How could you love such a bloody mess?" I ask myself.

"How could He love a mess such as me?" I answer.

Just as the husband didn't see what was right in front of him, it took me years to see the beauty of the crucifix beyond the blood, the pain and the wounds. Now I do. The reality of His reality has forever altered my reality.

Just as that elderly couple, frail and gray, could love each other more in their eighties than they did in their twenties, the Lord loves you. He's not consumed by outer appearances but by the inward appearance of the heart and the soul. The exterior things that matter to others don't matter to God. The interior parts we fear sharing with others are what God longs for us to share with Him.

Don't allow hurts, failures or pain from broken relationships with imperfect beings (even those you may have "loved at first sight") to dictate your openness to God, *the* Perfect Being, who loved you into sight, into existence. He loves you even more than you think possible. Appearance is just that: appearance.

Looks pass away, and beauty in the eyes of the world passes away, but true love is forever. Like most things Christian, it turns the world inside out.

SALVATION GIVEN

Charm is deceitful, and beauty is vain.

Proverbs 31:30

Love is not blind. True love, God's love, sees 20/20. It's the world that needs glasses.

How would Jesus like His eggs?

Take my yoke upon you and learn from me; for I am gentle and lowly in heart, and you will find rest for your souls. For my yoke is easy, and my burden is light.

Matthew 11:29–30

SITUATION EXPLAINED

Jesus must have eaten eggs. He shares his *yoke* with us.

SOLUTION OFFERED

Did you ever hear this Bible passage as a kid and think of egg yolks? I did. Every time I hear this reading from Matthew, I picture Jesus making an omelet. "I'ma let (*omelet*) you think 'bout that fer a minute 'er two," as one of my friends from the South often says to me. I'll wait while you *scramble* around for a dictionary that translates that into English.

One of the reasons we don't take more from this reading is that we don't completely understand Jewish culture. You see, Saint Matthew was a Jew writing to Jews about a Jew who claimed to be the King of the Jews, whom the Jews killed. (Read that again if you think it will help.) He didn't have to explain the design or purpose of the *yoke*. Since we live in a culture with the ability to flush a toilet and surf the Web, however, I'll take a minute to explain how it used to be.

A yoke (as many of you know) was the device that a person put around the head of an ox to tow the gear used to till the land. What many of us might not know, though, is that the yoke was usually built for two heads. It had two "slots" in it: for two oxen or for one ox and (if he only owned one ox) the farmer. That's right: the farmer would actually put his head through the yoke and pull the equipment, side by side with the ox.

When Jesus uttered this verse to the Jews, they understood that the yoke was built for two. They thereby understood that when Jesus said to "take [His] yoke," He meant that He and His followers would share the yoke. They would share their crosses.

Jesus does the same thing for us, offering to share our burdens each and every day. This is perfect for me, because it is only by the grace and help of Jesus that I don't get into trouble.

Once I learned about what a yoke was, I stopped associating this verse with eggs. You could say that I stepped out of my *shell*, saw the *whites* of Jesus' eyes and stopped looking for the *fluffy* answer in my daily walk. I don't want to sound too *hard-boiled*, but let's admit that before life is *over*, you'll find that it's not always *easy*. Oh, and if you don't get all of these puns *exactly*, just take a little time for *ketchup*.

If you take the yoke upon your shoulders, then God will call you, in a new way, to live on the *Son*ny side. Because Jesus rose *up* on Easter, no matter how you *color* it.

SALVATION GIVEN

Take my yoke upon you and learn from me; for I am gentle and lowly in heart, and you will find rest for your souls. For my yoke is easy, and my burden is light.

Matthew 11:29–30

Do you smell coffee? I thought we were reading from Matthew here, not "*He brews.*"

But who wants eggs without coffee?

Chapter Four

Encountering God During Ordinary Time

Embracing realities

No date on Valentine's Day?

He who does not love does not know God; for God is love.

1 John 4:8

SITUATION EXPLAINED

There's a true Lover in your life.

SOLUTION OFFERED

I can't stand Cupid. He's supposed to be this cute, cuddly, matchmaking angel, but that little guy annoys me. How insane is it that the universal (or at least American) symbol of love is a pudgy kid in diapers holding a lethal weapon, who is allowed to strike unsuspecting people at will with his aim of love?

Maybe I'm jealous, wishing that I were armed with a bow and arrow. Or maybe Cupid's arrow didn't hit enough for me during my high school years. Or maybe his arrow left more scars than happy memories.

All right, I got that out of my system.

Interestingly enough, Cupid comes to us from ancient mythology, where he was the god of erotic love, the son of Venus, goddess of love. *Erotic* comes from the Greek word *eros,* which means "the feeling of love." *Eros* is the word for temporary or fleeting love, based on emotion and momentary desire.

Now, as most people know, *erotic* is not a word that comes to mind when you envision pure love, God's love. For that there is another Greek word: *agape. Agape* love is unconditional love. That is the love that stands the test of time and of selfishness and that goes beyond emotions or moments. *Agape* love says, "I love you no matter what."

God loves you in an *agape* way. Jesus died for you in an *agape* way. The Spirit lives in you, allowing you to love in an *agape* way.

This world functions in mostly an *eros* love. It's not really love: it's "like" or "lust" without the commitment or the self-lessness. *Eros* love does not last. It uses and then it leaves.

Agape love, however, is not a "for now" love but a *forever* love. *Agape* love stands. It draws you and me closer to God with every breath.

Love is not symbolized by a boy in a loincloth carrying a weapon. Love is seen in a man covered in a loincloth nailed to a cross. His divine weapon is an *agape* love for you and for me.

Jesus doesn't strike unsuspecting people at will; His love strikes all people and challenges their wills. And His aim is as perfect as His love.

Women, you are someone's valentine, whether you feel like one or not. Jesus Himself, a man who calls other men to action, loves you more than you can imagine.

Men, whether or not you have a valentine, you are loved too. And you are called to be a man of God, like Jesus, loving in an *agape* rather than an *eros* way.

Cupid might be cute, but he's not the answer. Jesus Christ is the true "Love Master." Love is not about Valentine's Day but about Good Friday: That's the real day of love. Christians celebrate it not with candy or flowers but with their hearts.

SALVATION GIVEN

He who does not love does not know God; for God is love.

1 John 4:8

"*Cross* my heart" takes on a whole new meaning, huh?

Frustrated with life at home?

And Jesus said to them, "A prophet is not without honor, except in his own country, and among his own kin, and in his own house."

Mark 6:4

SITUATION EXPLAINED

Where is *the* most difficult place to act like a Christian?

SOLUTION OFFERED

I once read that over 80 percent of all automobile accidents happen within five miles of the person's home. This got me thinking. I'd submit that during the teenage years especially, over 80 percent of disagreements happen *within* our homes, sometimes on a daily basis. That doesn't mean we're horrible; it means we're human. Families can be really difficult at times.

Why then would God put us in a family? Is it His plan to drive us crazy? Couldn't He just as easily have made it so we lived alone? Well, He didn't. He knew that families are blessings too.

Why is that we can be patient and forgiving of friends or classmates or coworkers, even strangers on the street, but have a hard time acting Christian toward people living under our own roofs?

There are several possible reasons. One is that the people at home see us at our best and at our worst. It's difficult to hide our faults, bad habits and imperfections from family. It may be easy to paste on a smile for people at school, but it gets very difficult to do that with people who see you the minute you wake up or when you get home from a long day at work.

Sometimes we subconsciously think, "Hey, they're my family, so they have to forgive me." Other times we might be striving to be a good Christian example, but those who have known us since birth focus on who we were in the past rather than on who we're trying to become. This can deflate our efforts.

That's kind of what Jesus is experiencing in this passage. He has returned home after beginning His ministry elsewhere. The folks in Nazareth are having a difficult time believing that "little Jesus," whom they've known since His childhood, is returning as this incredible preacher and miracle-worker.

If you have experienced this kind of frustration at home, remember that Christ is the key. He knows what you're experiencing and wants to help you through it. Ask Him to grant you the strength, the wisdom and especially the patience to be a light to others, beginning in your own home.

Salvation Given

And Jesus said to them, "A prophet is not without honor, except in his own country, and among his own kin, and in his own house."

Mark 6:4

Christ: The best way to turn a house into a home.

Is your life a mess?

For on this day shall atonement be made for you, to cleanse you; from all your sins you shall be clean before the LORD.

Leviticus 16:30

SITUATION EXPLAINED

The soul often needs a spring cleaning, no matter what season it is. What's on your to-do list?

SOLUTION OFFERED

It struck me recently that I do a lot of "preventative maintenance" in my life. I change my oil every few thousand miles to keep my car running strong. I brush my teeth daily so that they don't fall out. I scandisk and de-frag my computer often to keep it running quickly.

I take the trash out at times before it gets full, so as not to stink up the place. I shower daily so I won't stink up the place.

Ever stop to think about all of the things you schedule in order to "keep running smoothly"?

So why is it weird or difficult to have the sacrament of reconciliation be a normally scheduled event in our faith walk as Catholic Christians? It is a necessary form of "upkeep," even more important than the list of physical maintenance activities.

I often find that "the spirit indeed is willing, but the flesh is weak" (Matthew 26:41). I let other things, far less important things, creep their way into my schedule and take the place of the most important thing: where I am in relationship with God.

The Leviticus verse is from the Old Testament, long before Christ gave the apostles the power to forgive sins in

His name (see Matthew 16:19; John 20:23). We can see very early (about 1400 BC) how God provides His children with ways to atone for sin and to "get straight" with Him.

Reconciliation is a perfect example of how a soul can drive the body. Of course, once the decision to take advantage of the sacrament is made, it's the body that needs to drive the soul to the church for reconciliation.

If it's not on the to-do list and hasn't been for a while, why not work it into the schedule? Catholics are uniquely blessed with the gift of the sacrament of reconciliation. We need to remember that it is not something to fear but something to cherish.

Go for it. Sit with Christ in this incredible sacrament, and *recon*nect in *recon*ciliation. You'll be glad you did.

SALVATION GIVEN

For on this day shall atonement be made for you, to cleanse you; from all your sins you shall be clean before the LORD.

Leviticus 16:30

Clear your calendar and do some spiritual *recon*naissance.

How can people cheat?

But you yourselves wrong and defraud, and that even your own brethren. Do you not know that the unrighteous will not inherit the kingdom of God?

1 Corinthians 6:8–9

SITUATION EXPLAINED

Do you know anybody who cheats?

SOLUTION OFFERED

Growing up, one of my older brothers was infamous for his cheating: swiping a few extra hundred dollars in Monopoly, hitting "reset" on the video games when he fell behind, dealing himself aces and "accidentally" bumping the game board and sending the pieces flying. You had to watch him every minute.

That kind of cheating isn't right, but it sure can be funny when you're a kid. Then there's the other kind of cheating, when people are intentionally dishonest. That kind of cheating is what this verse warns us against.

I've heard dishonest people try to justify cheating in school or cheating their bosses or the government. They try to spin the situation to make themselves look righteous and just in God's eyes. But there is nothing godly about dishonesty.

People have tried to take advantage of me because I'm a Christian. Maybe they think I am an idiot, or maybe they do it because they figure I have to forgive them. Whatever the case, they may or may not get away with it now, but they will have to answer for it eventually. The Scriptures promise us that.

It's really simple: God doesn't cheat, God doesn't create anyone to cheat, and He doesn't appreciate cheating. He expects honesty. Honorable people who act and work in good faith, with morals, are the ones of whom God is proud. They are the ones deserving of respect. You and I must always strive to be those people.

If you've ever been burned because of someone else's dishonesty, forgive and forget. But remember one thing: No one cheats God and gets away with it.

Salvation Given

But you yourselves wrong and defraud, and that even your own brethren. Do you not know that the unrighteous will not inherit the kingdom of God?

1 Corinthians 6:8–9

Cheaters never win, and winners never cheat.

Are you dealing with divorce in your family?

So take heed to yourselves, and let none be faithless to the wife of his youth. For I hate divorce, says the LORD the God of Israel.

Malachi 2:15–16

SITUATION EXPLAINED

Divorce is a challenge for the whole family.

SOLUTION OFFERED

This Scripture says it pretty clearly, huh? God hates divorce.

This is about as straightforward a verse from the Bible as you're going to get, one that is difficult to misinterpret. Unfortunately, it can leave divorced Catholics feeling as if the church does not welcome them or love them. Nothing could be further from the truth.

If your parents are divorced, know that God loves you and loves them; His love is not conditional. And if you've heard that the church doesn't accept divorced people, please let me apologize on behalf of my church for the miscommunication. Your family is loved—immensely.

Yes, this Scripture verse says that God hates divorce, but notice that it does not say that He hates divorced people. God does not hate His children, no matter what. Perfect love is incapable of hating the object of His love. He hates any*thing*—including sin, pride, selfishness and divorce— that inhibits our ability to give and receive love. But he does not hate any*one*.

Next, notice that His instruction is for His child to be faithful to his or her spouse, a vow that both the husband and wife swear to God and to one another by their own free will. God does not force them to do it. The priest performing the ceremony doesn't force them. The father of the bride doesn't force them, nor does the mother of the groom. God is calling the couple to honor their own commitment. If we do not do that, it's not God's fault but our own; it's not God's bad but ours.

Finally, notice that in order to be faithful to the bride, the groom must first "take heed to" himself. Basically, he must control himself. Obviously, the same is required of the bride. True self-control not only means controlling your own wants but also putting them second to the wants of God and the needs of the other. Think about that.

I've encountered many people in the past few years whose lives are wrought with pain because of divorce. Many of you feel that pain, I'm sure. It's difficult to discuss divorce because it is such an emotional topic. Reactions range from blame to guilt, from anger to numbness, from bitterness to rejection to outright hatred.

But it doesn't have to be that way. There are alternative ways to react.

Perhaps most important to remember is that it's not healthy to fall into the "blame game." Too often in divorce the energy goes into pointing out who was at fault in the past rather than on how to move forward in the future. That kind of focus is easy to get trapped in, but it's counterproductive.

This is especially true when children are involved. Sadly, some parents pit the results of their love (their children) against the former spouse. If this happens to you, you know well how frustrating it can be.

The best way for us to not only survive divorce but thrive

in spite of it is to spend less time trying to change others' minds and more time working on our own hearts. You can channel your energy into prayer and reading the Scriptures. Then you can find hope in this verse.

If your parents are divorced, realize a few things.

- It is not your fault, no matter what you might feel or even hear.
- Divorce does not stem from a lack of love between two people but a refusal or inability to love properly. The love that is required for a successful marriage in God is one rooted in self-sacrifice, and it takes more work than you can possibly imagine until you are married yourself. If one partner or both are unwilling to make the necessary sacrifices, the whole foundation crumbles.
- Your parents are suffering the effects of divorce too. They love you and want the best for you.
- Friends who haven't dealt with divorce firsthand may not quite understand your situation. They don't understand how difficult a holiday celebration or a weekend visit can become. That doesn't make them bad; it makes them fortunate.
- You are still blessed. God has a plan for you, and it extends beyond what you presently see or know.

Notice that God is calling *you* to avoid divorce, and He's giving an outline on how to do so. You need to be faithful to your future spouse, and you can be faithful only by practicing self-control.

Being faithful means that you don't date (or marry) people who lead you into sin. It means that you honor your commitment to your spouse even now by not giving away the gift of your sexuality to anyone else. Being faithful means that you are going to live for the other more than for yourself, putting him or her first (as Christ did for the church: see Ephesians 5).

Now, you might be saying to yourself, "Yes, but I've seen people give all of themselves and the other just takes advantage. It still ends in divorce, so how can I trust another?"

It's true that sometimes one person takes advantage of the one who is trying to do the right thing. But that is not a true marriage. A relationship that is "lopsided in love" is not a healthy one; do not make a commitment that is not mutual. Marriage is a covenant that promises to put the other first in all things.

Concentrate this day on being faithful to God and to your future spouse (if you are called to marriage), and do so by controlling your desires. Seek to serve others, and serving your spouse will be easier. Believe me.

And remember that your first love should always be God Himself. If you can keep that love first and foremost in your mind and heart, you'll come to understand why God hates divorce. God loves us, and He gives us marriage to reveal and model that love. His marriage to us is pure, faithful, everlasting, and He wants our marriages to reflect that.

SALVATION GIVEN

So take heed to yourselves, and let none be faithless to the wife of his youth. For I hate divorce, says the LORD the God of Israel.

Malachi 2:15–16

God loves you and your family, for better or for worse, as long as you both shall live. Love Him back.

Do you know anyone who is considering an abortion?

Henceforth all generations will call me blessed.

Luke 1:48

SITUATION EXPLAINED

We can look at the life of Mary and see how life's hardships can become life's blessings.

SOLUTION OFFERED

Would the world today, or even back then, really consider Mary's life blessed? I mean, think about it.

She is told she will bear a child out of wedlock, which was a capital crime and punishable by death. She travels hundreds of miles late in her pregnancy, atop a donkey, and gives birth without painkillers in poor and less-than-antiseptic conditions. She and her family are then forced to retreat hundreds of miles south for fear of their child's life.

Mary's son later "runs away," and she and Joseph have to search for him for three days. She then suffers the death of her husband, watches her only son leave home for good, then follows Him only to helplessly watch as He is unfairly convicted, maligned, beaten, mocked, tortured and put to death in the most brutal way imaginable.

Yet Mary was blessed?

A life like this nowadays would leave a mother feeling abandoned, cursed, angry or all three. But Mary is the perfect example of trust and of love.

Mary can relate to all women and all women to Mary, especially fear-filled young mothers. She too was a teenage mother uncertain about what the future held and aware of the possible social judgment awaiting her. As a young mother she endured hardship to protect her child.

In all this Mary was the perfect Christian disciple. She said, "Let it be to me according to your word" (Luke 1:38). It sure sounds a lot like "Thy kingdom come. Thy will be done" (Matthew 6:10), doesn't it?

As Mary did, we are called to live like Christ, who came so that we might have life (see John 10:10), not bring death.

How intimately does Christ know the fear and uncertainty of a young pregnant mother? Mary no doubt shared her heart with Him concerning the events surrounding His birth.

How passionately does He love women? He created and blessed them with the ability to participate uniquely in creation, to bring life into this world and to nurture it.

Mary endured great hardship to ensure that Christ, alive and growing in her womb, would live and fulfill the mission that God had for Him. We are called to do the same. Christ has a vocation and mission for all life, including the unborn.

In the mind and heart of God...

- is a twenty-year-old's life worth less than a sixty-year-old's?
- is a five-year-old's life worth less than a thirty-year-old's?
- is a life in the womb worth less than a life outside the womb?

The answers are obvious. If you disagree, sit down with a mother who has given birth and ask her.

Mary is blessed *for* her faithfulness, and you and I are blessed *by* her faithfulness. Her life gave life to His life, and His life exists in all life. We need to honor life and protect it, just as Mary did.

SALVATION GIVEN

Henceforth all generations will call me blessed.

Luke 1:48

Hardship can only become blessing when we realize what life is all about. Who is the author of life: we or He?

Do you struggle with an addiction?

And they bound him and led him away.

Matthew 27:2

SITUATION EXPLAINED

The man who was bound came to set us free.

SOLUTION OFFERED

Would you let an ant control your life? Would you let a fly dictate where you went? Would you let a worm cause you intense pain? Of course not. If any one of those tiny creatures tried any of those things, you'd probably squash it in an instant, because you're a whole lot bigger than it is and a lot smarter too.

Imagine how Jesus felt being beaten, mocked and tied up. He probably wore a collar that attached to his waist, as was common for criminals of that time. The collar would have caused Him to hunch over, almost bowing to His captors.

Jesus was chained and led around by His own creation, people He had breathed into existence, people He could breathe out of existence if He chose to do so. He could have broken the chains. He could have called upon legions of angels to level the city and reduce every person there to dust.

He didn't—because of you and your sin. He didn't—because of the people you love and their sin. Jesus took the form of a slave (see Philippians 2:7) so that you could be free.

It was totally backward. G-o-d was treated like a d-o-g. He allowed it to happen to Him so that it wouldn't have to happen to us. Unfortunately, though, it still does happen to us—through addictions.

Addictions are the dog collars that lead us down paths of misery. Addictions to image or weight loss destroy our bodies. Addictions to drugs and alcohol destroy our present and our futures. Addictions to pornography destroy families and relationships. Addictions to sex and masturbation destroy our ability to love. Put simply, addictions destroy our lives and our souls.

People in Alcoholics Anonymous sometimes get looked down upon when their humility ought to be praised. Many people with alcohol problems never have the courage to admit them and seek help, because they consider themselves "functional" in their habit.

Many pornography addicts refuse to admit that their addiction hurts anyone. That's a lie; it hurts everyone. Viewing God's creation in such a disordered way affects how they relate to others, their own sexuality and the dignity of the human body in general.

We bind ourselves to our addictions. The fire of our hearts illuminates paths that lead us *away* from God rather than to Him. But it does not have to be that way. Jesus *does* give us a way out of our addictions. Our souls can lead our bodies. It begins with us but ends with Him.

Jesus took on our sin so that we would no longer have to be bound by it. He gives us a choice, a chance at freedom. Make no mistake: Even if you have turned down that option for freedom thousands of times, the choice is still yours today to be free.

The collar of sin can come off, and the chains of addiction can be smashed. All you need to do is call upon God and avail yourself of His grace. We Catholics do so through the sacrament of reconciliation. The grace and mercy of Jesus is waiting for you; run to it.

Addiction is a tool of the devil, but it is rendered powerless when attacked with grace. The devil is not scared of you, but he is petrified of the presence of God within you. He cowers at the mere name of Jesus Christ. Unleash God's life (grace) and watch "Satan fall like lightning" once again (see Luke 10:18; John 12:31; Revelation 12:9).

While an addiction might seem way too big for you to handle, remember that it is *not* too big for God. In addition to the grace He offers in the sacraments, there are many good Alcoholics Anonymous and other twelve-step groups that are founded on His principles of honesty, repentance and forgiveness. Seek God's help and the help of your brothers and sisters.

SALVATION GIVEN

And they bound him and led him away.

Matthew 27:2

Don't allow the ant or the fly to "bug" you anymore. Seek the freedom of God. You might as well face it: God's addicted to love.

In sickness and in health?

Husbands, love your wives, as Christ loved the Church and gave himself up for her.

Ephesians 5:25

SITUATION EXPLAINED

Jesus is married—in a manner of speaking.

SOLUTION OFFERED

I was given an incredible gift not too long ago. My mom was admitted to the hospital.

You're probably thinking I'm a terrible son based on those first two sentences, but bear with me.

There I sat in a sterile white hospital room. The sounds of health care filled the germ-ridden air around me: doctors were being paged, phones ringing, machines beeping, nurses buzzing around. I watched as my mother was poked and prodded with needles. I looked helplessly at all of the tubes connected to her.

It was in this scene of uneasiness and pain that I was given the incredible gift. It was not one of those obvious gifts that come adorned in colorful wrapping paper on Christmas or your birthday. No, this was a gift that will never grow old, never fade, never lose its beauty and never, ever be forgotten.

The gift was in seeing the amazing love that my father has for my mother still today, stronger now than on the day they were married forty years ago. For he sat there too, also helpless, looking at his bride and wishing he could take away her pain. I noticed his immovable posture, his vigilance at his wife's bedside.

Then it hit me: *This* is how Christ loves us; *this* is how deeply and sincerely Jesus loves His bride, the church—you and me. The verse from Ephesians 5 echoed in my head.

Christ is the husband looking at His bride, wanting to take our pain away. Christ is the faithful spouse who takes that pain upon His own shoulders in the shape of a cross. Jesus looks right into our eyes, yours and mine, and says that there is no need for tears. The Lord will never leave our side.

I am better capable of loving today than I was before I saw my father's example of love. The more faithful we are to our spouse, Jesus Christ, and the more we seek to love Him above anyone else, the more others will see that love in our eyes and the better they will be able to love. The pattern will keep repeating itself: It's an outward sign and a perfect circle, just like the wedding ring.

My mother is out of the hospital now, thank God, and back at home with her husband.

Life may get back to normal, but things are not the same: not in their marriage, not in my family and not in my relationship with Jesus Christ.

Sometimes it takes pain and suffering to really see the love. Look no further than Calvary. What happened on that cross two thousand years ago was the greatest "I do" in history.

SALVATION GIVEN

Husbands, love your wives, as Christ loved the Church and gave himself up for her.

Ephesians 5:25

Marriage is not about finding someone you can live with but about finding someone you cannot live without.

Are you ready to die?

Watch therefore, for you know neither the day nor the hour.

Matthew 25:13

SITUATION EXPLAINED

Do you just *assume* you're going to wake up tomorrow, that there's plenty of time left to do what you want to do and say what you want to say?

SOLUTION OFFERED

Recently I've lost two friends. One moved away, and the other passed away. I wasn't prepared to lose either of them. There were things that I wanted to tell both of them that I didn't get chances to say.

People are always telling us to "live each day as if it were your last." Good advice. The problem is that a lot of us say it but forget to do it. Even worse is when we say it but then live in the wrong way. We act in selfish and sinful ways, believing it is OK because "we only live once."

But living each day as if it is our last does not mean doing whatever we want or whatever makes us happy. It means living each moment in a way that pleases God. It means running *to* God rather than away from Him. It means doing what's right in God's eyes, not in the eyes of our peers.

If it is all over today, are you ready? If God whispered to you right now, "Today is your last," would you live today the same way you had planned? I'd probably live today a little differently—actually, a lot differently.

Is there anything you want or need to say to God or to someone else? Remember this Scripture encouraging you to be prepared.

Don't let another day go by without telling those who mean the most to you how you feel about them. Don't assume that there's plenty of time, because you do only live once. Make God proud!

Speaking for myself, I think I have a few people to call. What about you?

SALVATION GIVEN

Watch therefore, for you know neither the day nor the hour.

Matthew 25:13

God doesn't give a lot of warning all the time. He acts. He's allowed. He's God.

Are you wondering about your future?

Having the eyes of your hearts enlightened, that you may know what is the hope to which he has called you.

Ephesians 1:18

SITUATION EXPLAINED

Are you wondering what you are going be when you grow up? I'm an adult, and I still wonder.

SOLUTION OFFERED

What did God create you to do? Are you doing it? If not, are you on your way? If not, then why not?

What if Walt Disney had been afraid of mice?

What if the Dairy Queen had been lactose intolerant?

What if Dr. Pepper hadn't gone to medical school?

What if Betsy Ross had said, "Sewing is stupid"?

What if Henry Ford had been content walking everywhere?

What if Amelia Earhart had been afraid of flying?

What if Michael Jordan had ignored basketball and tried some other sport? (Yeah, right!)

What if Joan of Arc had said, "Fighting is strictly a man's job"?

What if Beethoven didn't want to take piano lessons?

What if Rosa Parks had allowed fear to tempt her out of that bus seat?

What if Abraham Lincoln had decided to stay on the farm instead of going to school?

What if Mother Teresa had said, "One person can't make a difference"?

What if Karol Wojtyla had pursued soccer as a profession instead of entering the seminary? We would never have known him as Pope John Paul II, a man through whom God worked miracles and changed the face of the modern world.

I wonder how many people have ignored God's call to greatness due to fear, pride or selfishness. Are *we* open to what and where God calls us, regardless of the consequences?

For instance, God is calling priests, nuns and brothers today. Some are answering the call; some are not. Have you ever thought about it? Does it scare you? God can work through fear.

It was once said that our talents are our gifts from God, and what we do with our talents are our gifts back to God. What's holding you back? Don't let it. Your prayerful focus will determine your future.

Salvation Given

Having the eyes of your hearts enlightened, that you may know what is the hope to which he has called you.

Ephesians 1:18

I hope that one day a young Catholic will say, "What if the Bible Geek® had never picked up that Bible?"

And if that day ever comes, Lord, I'll know we're just getting started.

Does the Word of God ever confuse you?

If we endure, we shall also reign with him;
if we deny him, he also will deny us.

2 Timothy 2:12

SITUATION EXPLAINED

Are you looking at God's Word or your word?

SOLUTION OFFERED

Those game shows on television drive me crazy. Every once in a while I watch one for a minute or two. I can't stand them—not because of the overexcited people or the lame sets, but because I always get questions wrong that I actually know the answer to. Why, you may ask? Because I second-guess.

Have you ever felt that the answer to a question just seems *too* easy? It's an amazing phenomenon. In an ordinary conversation you wouldn't even think about a certain fact, but when you put it in the context of a question (that is slowly read), you begin to think too much and stop trusting your natural instincts.

You begin wondering,

Did Shakespeare really write *Hamlet?*
Is Iceland actually a country?
Am I sure you spell *kitchen* with a "t"?
Were there seven dwarves, or were there twelve?
What is my name?

Sometimes things are so simple that we have a hard time believing them. The same can be true of Scripture.

Often people get confused while reading the Bible because the God they are encountering is not consistent with the God whom they have created in their heads. They wonder why God acts the way He does or says some of the things that He does.

What's worse is that next, rather than seeking to find out why, many people simply dismiss God's words as outdated, symbolic or unimportant. They keep the parts of Scripture that make them feel good and dismiss the parts that challenge them or fill them with uneasiness.

One reason that the God of the Bible doesn't seem consistent with the God to whom people pray is because they haven't gotten to know Him personally. They see the Bible as so intimidating or boring that they never open it. They never get to read verses like this one, which, while challenging, sums up the promise of living as a Christian.

If we believe the Bible to be the Word *of* God and not simply words *about* Him, then we are left with two choices:

1) We believe what we think about God.
2) We believe what God tells us about Himself.

I know which one I'm going to choose.

SALVATION GIVEN

If we endure we shall also reign with him;
if we deny him, he also will deny us.

2 Timothy 2:12

Mark Twain claimed, "It ain't those parts of the Bible that I can't understand that bother me, it is the parts that I do understand."

While Mark wasn't a great Christian, he sure does make a good point if you read his quote through God's eyes.

You don't feel like acting Christian today?

But as for you, continue in what you have learned and have firmly believed, knowing from whom you learned it.

2 Timothy 3:14

SITUATION EXPLAINED

Do you have a bad memory at times?

SOLUTION OFFERED

I have so much to learn about life, love, the world, God— the list seems to be endless. There are several things that I seem to have to learn over and over again. Sometimes that's OK; there are fundamental truths that we can never hear too often.

As I was reflecting on some of my favorite passages from Scripture, I began to see a strand of universal truths that I occasionally forget or take for granted. While this list is in no way complete, and may vary greatly from yours, it is a starting point. I hope you can relate.

Ten things the Bible teaches me that I keep forgetting:

1. God loves me, no matter what (Romans 8:38–39).
2. God is not some impersonal being; He is my Father (Galatians 4:6).
3. Jesus shows His power through His humility (Philippians 2:8).
4. Through the Holy Spirit anything is possible (Luke 1:37).
5. We are never alone; God is always with us (Matthew 28:20).
6. The devil exists and wants to take my eyes off God (Romans 7:21).

7. God will always give us what we *need* (Psalm 10:17).

8. Prayer works; God can change everything, even our families (Psalm 32:6).

9. Wisdom is a powerful weapon, one that we can and should pray for (James 1:5).

10. Heaven is *so* worth the wait (1 Corinthians 2:9).

I might forget a thousand things in the course of a week: phone numbers, names, PINs. But if I can remember these ten truths, I'm in good shape. I'm equipped to wake up, face the world and walk my walk.

You will be too. Commit these ten, or ten of your own, to memory, and trust that God is present and active in your life. God is waiting, and He is willing to work a miracle through you today. Let Him.

Salvation Given

But as for you, continue in what you have learned and have firmly believed, knowing from whom you learned it.

2 Timothy 3:14

The Bible: God's greatest gift to those of us who need a "reminder" from time to time.

Chapter Five

Encountering God All the Time
Finding Him in the first place you look

Does your pillow change temperature?

The LORD preserves the simple.

Psalm 116:6

SITUATION EXPLAINED

In a given week I enjoy many simple pleasures that make me smile.

SOLUTION OFFERED

It was once said that life's greatest pleasures are often the simplest ones. For me, one of the greatest pleasures on this earth is the cold pillow.

You know the feeling. You wake up from a deep sleep, still tired. You reposition yourself in the bed and prepare to fall back asleep, but before you do, you flip over your pillow. Aaaaahhh. The cool side is waiting to welcome you, and thank God it does.

The cold pillow is a simple pleasure that makes an already great sleep experience even better. Who knows how it happens? It is just one of the inexplicable phenomena of our universe, I guess. All I know is that I like it.

Come to think of it, some of God's greatest gifts to me are the simplest ones:

- my dogs waiting for me at the door
- a really good slice of pizza
- sleeping in
- a long hot shower
- hugs from my little girls
- a first-class upgrade on the plane (rare but awesome)
- eating buffalo wings with my buddies

- an e-mail that says, "Thanks"
- fresh-smelling sheets on the bed
- a great confession
- spending time in Adoration
- reading my Bible on top of a mountain at sunset
- kissing my wife, the woman of my dreams

Look at your day or week. Where have your simplest pleasures been lately?

Life can be complicated at times. Far too often, though, we are the ones who complicate it. Maybe it's time to simplify your life. Recognize the little things that bring you joy, and thank God for them.

SALVATION GIVEN

The LORD preserves the simple.

Psalm 116:6

Life may not be easy, but it can be simple if you let it.

Are you a heavy sleeper?

He will not let your foot be moved,
*   he who keeps you will not slumber.*
Behold, he who keeps Israel
*   will neither slumber nor sleep.*

                                    Psalms 121:3–4

SITUATION EXPLAINED

Sleeping can be a great form of prayer (well, sort of).

SOLUTION OFFERED

Have you ever noticed in the Bible how many things—really important things—happen to people while they're sleeping? To name a few:

It was while he slept that the Lord took one of Adam's ribs and formed Eve (see Genesis 2:21).

It was in a dream that Jacob saw his vision of the ladder to heaven (see Genesis 28:12).

It was while the boy Samuel was lying down to rest for the night that the Lord called him to be His prophet (see 1 Samuel 3:9).

It was in a dream that the angel told Joseph not to fear and to take Mary as his wife (see Matthew 1:20).

Now, I don't want to get into dream analysis and all that stuff; I'll leave that to Joseph (the one in Genesis 40, not Jesus' stepdad). It is intriguing and important to point out, though, that God does not stop working in our lives when we go to sleep. As this verse reminds us, God doesn't need sleep.

We, on the other hand, need rest just as much as we need food, water and air. Too often sleep is the basic human necessity that we most quickly sacrifice. We'll push our bodies, minds and souls to the absolute limit, until we fall apart or make ourselves sick.

That is one of the reasons that God *commands* (not suggests) that we take time off and have a Sabbath day: not because He needs it but because we need it. Can you imagine how much better we would be as people, as families and as a church if we actually took one-seventh of our time and just rested, played and prayed? This world would look a lot different.

Go ahead, take the time. In fact, make the time. Give your body a good rest. You may not think you need it, but give it a try.

God will keep working while you are asleep. In fact, God might work in you in a new way. He might not remove one of your ribs or send an angel to stand before you, but your spirit will be renewed, refreshed and made ready to do His work.

SALVATION GIVEN

He will not let your foot be moved,
  he who keeps you will not slumber.
Behold, he who keeps Israel
  will neither slumber nor sleep.

Psalms 121:3–4

Having trouble sleeping? Don't count sheep; talk to the Shepherd.

Is your world noisy?

A great and strong wind tore the mountains, and broke in pieces the rocks before the LORD, but the LORD was not in the wind; and after the wind an earthquake, but the LORD was not in the earthquake; and after the earthquake a fire, but the LORD was not in the fire; and after the fire a still small voice.

1 Kings 19:11–13

SITUATION EXPLAINED

As you are reading these words, what sounds do you hear? Is it noisy or quiet where you are?

SOLUTION OFFERED

From the first annoying sounds of the alarm clock in the morning to the final phrases we hear from the television at night, the day can be an incessant flurry of audiowaves. We hear things—even beautiful things—from the stereo, the computer, the radio. Finding silence is difficult these days; some days almost impossible. Or is it?

Silence is not so much a treasure to be found as a necessity to be created (and cherished). Silence sometimes evades you and me because we are unwilling to let it find us in our overly busy schedules.

The truth is that we need silence in our lives. In fact, silence is one of the best communication media that God uses.

Take this verse, for instance. Here we have Elijah, one of the greatest of the prophets, and God leads him to the top of a mountain. There he witnesses the strong winds (strong enough to crush rocks), but God does not speak that way. He watches as the entire earth moves and quakes, and again, nothing. He sees the fire and its effects, but alas, God is not speaking to him in the fiery flames. Finally there is a whisper, and *that* is how the Lord communicates His message to His prophet.

Had there been any noise, Elijah would have missed God's message. He would have missed the opportunity to go and share that message with others.

If God were speaking to you in a whisper today, would you hear it? I have to admit that most days I would not. I am constantly looking for God in the great noises and big actions around me. Rarely do I shut up long enough for Him to whisper in my ear, into the silent depths of my heart.

Many of you, I know, can relate. I had a teenager tell me last week that a thirty-minute walk she took through nature was the first time she remembered being silent on purpose. A quiet walk can be a prayer, and that too is a gift.

Whether you are working or in school, on vacation or in the grind, one thing is certain: Silence is important, a commodity that we often do not take full advantage of, but should.

Make time to be silent today. Turn off the stereo when driving. Turn off the cell phone for a while. Take a walk away from technology, or head to bed early for a solid "rap session" with God, one in which He does all of the talking.

God did not show Himself in the "big ways," even to one of His greatest prophets. He showed up in a whisper. Elijah learned to listen for it. Will you?

SALVATION GIVEN

A great and strong wind tore the mountains, and broke in pieces the rocks before the LORD, but the LORD was not in the wind; and after the wind an earthquake, but the LORD was not in the earthquake; and after the earthquake a fire, but the Lord was not in the fire; and after the fire a still small voice.

1 Kings 19:11–13

Have a "silent night" with God.

Therefore I intend always to remind you of these things, though you know them and are established in the truth that you have....And I will see to it that after my departure you may be able at any time to recall these things.

2 Peter 1:12, 15

SITUATION EXPLAINED

Do you ever repeat something to yourself so you won't forget it, like a telephone number?

SOLUTION OFFERED

Once, when I was a child and I left the door open behind me (in the middle of summer), my mother asked me, "What? Were you born in a barn?"

"No, but Jesus was," I replied. I grew to love the taste of soap.

To this day that question reminds me of that day, but more to the point, in a weird way it reminds me of Jesus. Words and phrases can do that if we let them. We can assign meanings and associations to them that will draw our attention, our minds and our hearts back to God, right in the middle of an everyday conversation.

In this verse we have Peter showing the importance of reminding ourselves to remember God in all things, in order to have Him on our minds constantly. With that idea in mind, I compiled a list of some famous phrases that you might hear from time to time, along with some of the Scriptures that run through my head when I hear them:

The grass is always greener on the other side.

"While yet in flower and not cut down,

they wither before any other plant." (Job 8:12)

Where there's smoke there's fire.

"And Mount Sinai was wrapped in smoke, because the LORD descended upon it in fire" (Exodus 19:18).

They don't see eye to eye.

"You hypocrite, first take the log out of your own eye, and then you will see clearly to take the speck out of your brother's eye" (Matthew 7:5).

I call 'em like I see 'em.

"My brethren, if any one among you wanders from the truth and some one brings him back, let him know that whoever brings back a sinner from the error of his way will save his soul from death and will cover a multitude of sins" (James 5:19–20).

Let sleeping dogs lie.

"His watchmen are blind,
    they are all without knowledge;
they are all mute dogs,
    they cannot bark;
dreaming, lying down,
    loving to slumber." (Isaiah 56:10)

A rolling stone gathers no moss.

"And they were saying to one another, 'Who will roll away the stone for us from the door of the tomb?'" (Mark 16:3).

Blood is thicker than water.

"Moses and Aaron did as the LORD commanded; in the sight of Pharaoh and in the sight of his servants, he lifted up the rod and struck the water that was in the Nile, and all the water that was in the Nile turned to blood" (Exodus 7:20–21).

If the shoe fits, wear it.

"And he preached, saying, 'After me comes he who is mightier than I, the thong of whose sandals I am not worthy to stoop down and untie. I have baptized you with water; but he will baptize you with the Holy Spirit'" (Mark 1:7–8).

When I was your age...

"When I was a child, I spoke like a child, I thought like a child, I reasoned like a child; when I became a man, I gave up childish ways" (1 Corinthians 13:11).

Take it one day at a time.

"For a day in your courts is better
    than a thousand elsewhere." (Psalm 84:10)

At least you've got your health.

"For I will restore health to you,
    and your wounds I will heal,
            says the LORD" (Jeremiah 30:17).

Love can build a bridge.

"And through him to reconcile to himself all things, whether on earth or in heaven, making peace by the blood of his cross" (Colossians 1:20).

SALVATION GIVEN

Therefore I intend always to remind you of these things, though you know them and are established in the truth that you have....And I will see to it that after my departure you may be able at any time to recall these things.

2 Peter 1:12, 15

If you can remember movie lines and song lyrics, you can remember Scripture.

Don't you hate paper cuts?

For the word of God is living and active, sharper than any two-edged sword, piercing to the division of soul and spirit, of joints and marrow, and discerning the thoughts and intentions of the heart.

Hebrews 4:12

SITUATION EXPLAINED

Has the Word of God cut into you lately?

SOLUTION OFFERED

One of the most painful, most annoying displeasures in all of humanity has to be the paper cut. How something so trivial as paper can inflict such an aggravating wound is beyond me.

You've all been there. You're working productively, furiously shuffling papers around, when all of a sudden, "OUCH! Great googly-moogly!" (or something to that effect).

The only thing worse than getting one of those really deep paper cuts (the kind that don't heal for a while) is having a band-aid that doesn't stay on and getting something like ketchup, salsa or lemon juice in the cut. That really hurts!

I've even gotten a paper cut from turning a page in my Bible. Who knew that the Word of God could be so dangerous, huh? Well, actually, anyone who has ever *really* read it knows how it can cut you, which in essence is what this passage from Hebrews is telling us.

This verse is one of my favorites in all of the sacred Scriptures. It says so many things. It reminds us that the Word is of *God*, the Creator of all creation. His Word not only exists but is living and effective, not dead and useless.

The verse goes further, comparing the Word to a sword. This analogy was very powerful to readers in the time after Christ. They lived in a country and world constantly at war. Those who were skillful with a sword could dismantle an opponent, any opponent, in a matter of seconds.

The Word, however, "cuts deeper" than even that. It is even more exacting and more penetrating of us and of our hearts. When you and I take the time, sit down and read the Scriptures, we begin to see ourselves the way that God sees us.

The words of the Bible, particularly the Gospels, cut through the pride, insecurities and masks of this life as a scalpel cuts through flesh. They reveal the interior of our bodies: our true hearts. The Word of God, when read honestly and sincerely, shows us who our God is and what our false gods are. The Bible will show us our true condition.

As a great author once noted, the Bible is not the antidote but the X ray. It points out problem areas. Christ is the doctor, and He specializes in "internal medicine." He wants to heal and to perfect all He has exposed through the Word.

Paper cuts can run deep, but there are steps we can take to alleviate the pain. The Word of God might "hurt" too, but this pain doesn't have to last a long time either. The doctor is waiting to heal. All you have to do is call on Him.

Salvation Given

For the word of God is living and active, sharper than any two-edged sword, piercing to the division of soul and spirit, of joints and marrow, and discerning the thoughts and intentions of the heart.

Hebrews 4:12

The Word of God is indeed living. Is it living in you *in deeds*?

Does God read the newspaper?

They received the word with all eagerness, examining the Scriptures daily to see if these things were so.

Acts 17:11

SITUATION EXPLAINED

Where do you get your news from?

SOLUTION OFFERED

I asked this riddle constantly when I was in elementary school. I know it's lame. You've probably either told or heard it yourself:

"What's black and white and red all over?"

That's right, the newspaper.

Although the Internet is quickly catching up, most people still get their daily news directly from the paper. It's good to stay informed about the world around us.

At the same time, I can point out many days when I opened the newspaper—written by men and women with all sorts of different motivations—and I did not open the Bible, God's inspired Word. How is it that I have time to read current events, check the weather and read the sports cover to cover but do not have five minutes to grow closer to God? The newspaper can't compare to the Bible.

You want *front-page* news?

The Bible has heroic rescues, families being reunited and courageous young people changing their worlds. And if you're one of those people fascinated by the darker side of the news, there's betrayal, lust, backstabbing, jealousy, heartbreak, intrigue and battle scenes that make *Ultimate Cage Fighting* look like an afternoon at a retirement home. Most importantly, if you read this book daily, you will hear about the real war that is going on and the effects it has on you (see 1 Peter 5:8).

You want *sports?*

The Bible has everything from wrestling (see Genesis 32:22–32) and fencing (see 1 Samuel 14) to fishing (see John 21:1–13), running and boxing (see 1 Corinthians 9:26–27). There's sailing (see Acts 27) and horseback riding (see Exodus 15:1, 19), too.

You want *weather?*

Get snow (see Isaiah 1:18; Daniel 3:50), hail (see Exodus 9:13–26), rain (see Job 36:27–29), sunshine (see Isaiah 18:4) and severe flooding (see Genesis 7). You'll also find out when the Son will rise.

You need to peruse the *money* section?

Don't be fooled; it's not in the book of Numbers. But you will find money discussed in Matthew 6:24, 1 Timothy 6:10 and elsewhere.

You want *government* or *politics?*

Look at 1 and 2 Kings and 1 and 2 Chronicles.

Oh, and are you looking through the *classifieds* for a career change?

Check out the book of *Job.*

And you like to read the *comics?*

There are plenty of animated characters in the Bible.

Want to know about the social scene or what happens on the *weekend?*

There's never been a more eventful Friday, Saturday and Sunday than what the Gospels record in their final chapters. Read all about it!

Searching for your *horoscope?*

Not necessary. You were born under the sign of the cross.

Want the *cross*word?

It's love.

The Bible *is* black and white and red all over. It is God's Word. It is truth. It is black and white in a world of gray. It is red, stained with the blood of Christ and with the blood of the millions who have given their lives defending its teaching, preaching it, upholding it and preserving it, that you and I might read it.

SALVATION GIVEN

They received the word with all eagerness, examining the Scriptures daily to see if these things were so.

Acts 17:11

Don't just read the news. Read the *Good News.*

Take another look at nursery rhymes

*For what great nation is there that has a god so near to it as the
LORD our God is to us, whenever we call upon him?...Only take
heed, and keep your soul diligently, lest you forget the things which
your eyes have seen, and lest they depart from your heart all the days
of your life; make them known to your children and your children's
children.*

Deuteronomy 4:7, 9

SITUATION EXPLAINED

In the United States we separate church and state, but the
reality is that God is everywhere. We Christians know where
to look.

SOLUTION OFFERED

Believe it or not, I learned about Jesus in public school; I just
didn't realize it. Maybe church and state are not as separate
as they seem.

Do you remember the nursery rhymes that came cour-
tesy of Mother Goose?

Mary had a little lamb, little lamb, little lamb;
Mary had a little lamb; its fleece was white as snow.
Everywhere that Mary went, Mary went, Mary went;
Everywhere that Mary went, the lamb was sure to go.

Well, the public school superintendents may not like this,
but this little rhyme sounds pretty biblical to me. Let me
show ya' what I mean:

"Mary, of whom Jesus was born, who is called Christ"
(Matthew 1:16).

"He looked at Jesus as he walked, and said, 'Behold,

the Lamb of God!'" (John 1:36).

"His appearance was like lightning, and his clothing white as snow" (Matthew 28:3). (Clothing in early Palestine was often referred to as "raiment" or "fleece.")

"Now his parents went up to Jerusalem every year at the feast of the Passover. And when he was twelve years old, they went up according to custom" (Luke 2:41–42).

"And the mother of Jesus was there; Jesus also was invited to the marriage" (John 2:1–2).

Mary did have a little Lamb, we call him Jesus, and His life was as white and pure as snow. Jesus often was in the company of Mary, teaching us both respect for and obedience to our mother, as a good older brother does.

Robert Fulghum gave his book of essays the catchy title *All I Really Need to Know I Learned in Kindergarten* (Ballantine, 2003). Maybe he's right. In kindergarten we learn to read, to write, to count. We learn to share, to listen and to respect others. We learn to play and to rest. We learn the most basic survival skills, really: patience, kindness and humility. These are all Christian virtues, the keys that unlock the doors to life in its later stages.

Thank God for simple nursery rhymes that remind us of all that is good and of just how simple the most profound truths of life can be. Virtues are rooted in Christ; they are "elementary" in that they are simple ideals that are taught, publicly and privately.

I am thankful for all those who hold virtues and values dear, especially those who teach them to our young. They make a difference, and I'm sorry that I didn't realize it sooner. God bless them all.

SALVATION GIVEN

For what great nation is there that has a god so near to it as the LORD our God is to us, whenever we call upon him?...Only take heed, and keep your soul diligently, lest you forget the things which your eyes have seen, and lest they depart from your heart all the days of your life; make them known to your children and your children's children.

Deuteronomy 4:7, 9

Let's close with a rhyme:

> Mary, my Mother,
> gave birth to my brother,
> who is like no other:
> Jesus, my Lord.

Do you have to do the dishes?

I will wipe Jerusalem as one wipes a dish, wiping it and turning it upside down.

2 Kings 21:13

SITUATION EXPLAINED

Great meal, Mom! Dishes? Me?

SOLUTION OFFERED

I was blessed with hardworking parents, and our family never had to worry about there being food on the table. Looking back now, it amazes me how bratty I could be back then, especially after dinner. I would finish a great dinner that I did not even help prepare and, with a full stomach, complain about doing the dishes. Didn't my father understand that I had other more important things to do, like watching television, playing video games, digesting and burping?

This verse from 2 Kings (not exactly a book that most people read on a daily basis, me included) is one that can teach us a lot, even twenty-seven hundred years later. God speaks this message through a prophet to the folks living in Jerusalem, people who were blessed by God but who then turned their backs and refused to serve Him. Kind of like me, little brats who had been blessed but then were selfish about serving.

If you sometimes catch yourself thinking that the Bible is "just a bunch of stories" with no real-life application, think again. God knows us so well and wants so much for us to relate to Him in understandable terms that He often comes to us and speaks to us in very common, everyday ways, using examples like doing the dishes.

Small acts of service, often unnoticed, are great ways to live the Scriptures, bringing the words to life. The Father feeds us at the table, and we never go hungry. In return, He asks that His children serve one another.

Next time you eat dinner at home, take the time afterward to do the dishes. Some people might drop dead from shock, others may not notice, but be assured that your heavenly Dad does.

SALVATION GIVEN

I will wipe Jerusalem as one wipes a dish, wiping it and turning it upside down.

2 Kings 21:13

The only time they didn't do dishes was the Last Supper, because He was about to perform an even greater act of service.

Thank you, Jesus.

Do you read those street signs?

Teach me to do your will,
  for you are my God!
Let your good spirit lead me
  on a level path!

Psalm 143:10

SITUATION EXPLAINED

Take another look at those street signs you see every day. They can tell you more.

SOLUTION OFFERED

God speaks to us in a variety of ways each day—some obvious, some not-so-obvious. It may be through His Word or through prayer. He might speak through leaders, parents or even through children. His voice might come to you through a phone call or an e-mail.

In what ways has God been trying to speak to you lately? What signs has He used?

This verse from Psalms expresses a desire to know God's will, which implies putting our will second to His. To do that takes an awareness of the ways in which He speaks to us and to the signs He uses to guide us.

Driving around the past few days, I've noticed several signs that could apply to our daily faith walk:

One sign warns us to *turn around,* even if we don't want to. "So shun youthful passions and aim at righteousness, faith, love, and peace, along with those who call upon the Lord from a pure heart" (2 Timothy 2:22).

A sign warns us not to be *closed* to the truth. "For this people's heart has grown dull, / and their ears are heavy of hearing, / and their eyes they have closed" (Matthew 13:15).

Another sign tells us *no trespassing*, but God offers us a way out of our failure to heed it. "For if you forgive men their trespasses, your heavenly Father also will forgive you" (Matthew 6:14).

Another sign reminds us of the *speed limit*. "Let every man be quick to hear, slow to speak, slow to anger" (James 1:19).

Another sign orders us to *stop* our selfish ways. "Judge not, and you will not be judged; condemn not, and you will not be condemned" (Luke 6:37).

A sign tells us which way needs to *yield* to avoid danger. "Incline not my heart to any evil, / to busy myself with wicked deeds" (Psalm 141:4).

A sign invites us to *merge* our will to God's and not to the world. "Do not be conformed to this world but be transformed by the renewal of your mind, that you may prove what is the will of God, what is good and acceptable and perfect" (Romans 12:2).

A sign encourages us to *stay straight* when temptations arise. "Lead me, O LORD, in your righteousness...; / make your way straight before me" (Psalm 5:8).

A sign reminds us that we are *under construction*. "So put away all malice and all guile and insincerity and envy and all slander. Like newborn infants, long for the pure spiritual milk, that by it you may grow up to salvation" (1 Peter 2:1–2).

Where are the signs in your life? Are you willing to let God direct your path?

SALVATION GIVEN
Teach me to do your will,

for you are my God!
Let your good spirit lead me
on a level path!

Psalm 143:10

I have to go read my Bible some more. I'm in the middle of a *crosswalk* (see Luke 9:23).

Listen to me,...

    and bud like a rose growing by a stream of water;
send forth fragrance...,

    and put forth blossoms....

 Scatter the fragrance, and sing a hymn of praise;

  bless the Lord for all his works,

...

with songs on your lips.

Sirach 39:13–15

SITUATION EXPLAINED

How did a dozen fresh, long-stem, red roses become a common way to symbolize love?

SOLUTION OFFERED

Many women say that it lacks creativity. Many men complain that they are too expensive.

Many people claim a card can say more. But I have yet to meet a woman who hates getting a dozen red roses delivered.

It's always nice to have someone think of you, especially when it isn't an anniversary. It means a lot when flowers arrive "just because someone loves you" and not because the person "has to do it."

Which gets me thinking, why are twelve red roses the norm to demonstrate our love for another? Why not a basket of fruit? Of course, then I remember how the fruit idea turned out for our lovebirds in Eden.

Why not a half dozen or two dozen? Why red roses and not white? Why not daffodils or daisies?

When it comes to the Bible, roses are almost never mentioned because, as any Scripture scholar will tell you, roses are not very common in Israel. Still, I like to remember that all creation points us back to its Creator, and so I wondered, "How could this commonly accepted symbol of love symbolize Love in the flesh, Jesus Christ?"

Why flowers? Perhaps to remind us that although it was in a garden that sin entered the world, it was also in a garden, outside a tomb, where we were assured that death was destroyed forever.

Why do they have to be fresh? Perhaps to remind us of the smell of the burial spices and perfumes that lingered in the empty tomb. Perhaps to make us want to lead better lives in what the saints call "the fragrance of God's holiness."

Why are there a dozen? Perhaps for the twelve apostles, or perhaps for the Blessed Virgin Mary, one for every star with which she is now crowned (see Revelation 12:1).

Why are they red? Perhaps to remind us of the beautiful blood poured out on that cross.

Why the long stem? Perhaps to remind us that it takes time to get to the prize, or maybe to help us feel connected to the life-giving water when we go through spiritual dryness.

Why are they delivered? Perhaps because we are delivered from our sins. Jesus gave the greatest sign of His love on Good Friday. His cross is like unexpected flowers in that it shows He was thinking of you. But the cross is not a one-time remembrance of you or a token gift because it was a holiday. It is the ultimate reminder of His love.

Finally, why *roses* of all the kinds of flowers? Why not a *Son*flower?

Well, that one is easy. We're always asking, "What would Jesus do?" Well, on Easter Sunday morning, the Lord *rose*.

Of course, the hard part is that everyone wants the roses but no one wants the thorns; everyone wants heaven but nobody wants to die. God, the rose's Creator, didn't design it that way though. Jesus *rose* on Easter Sunday, but not before He endured Friday's *thorns*.

Maybe a dozen red roses can be a thoughtful gift. It's all in how you look at them. The cross of Christ is certainly a loving gift. It comes with a card with your name on it, and it says, "Because I love you."

SALVATION GIVEN

Listen to me,...
    and bud like a rose growing by a stream of water;
send forth fragrance...,
    and put forth blossoms....
 Scatter the fragrance, and sing a hymn of praise;
    bless the Lord for all his works,

...

with songs on your lips.

                                  Sirach 39:13–15

Roses die, but Jesus lives forever.

Would Jesus play video games?

I am the living bread which came down from heaven; if any one eats of this bread, he will live forever; and the bread which I shall give for the life of the world is my flesh.

John 6:51

SITUATION EXPLAINED

Do you remember Pac-Man? I think he was a Catholic.

SOLUTION OFFERED

I loved video games growing up. I spent more time with that old black-and-white television in our basement than with any other piece of furniture in the house. For one summer, though, all but one of my video games gathered dust. That was the summer that I was introduced to Pac-Man.

Pac-Man was as close to "stress" as an eight-year-old could get. The formula was mind-boggling: one maze, one man, four ghosts and all of those little pellets to eat. As the rounds progressed, the evil ghosts would get faster and faster, and it became increasingly difficult to make it through the maze without dying.

That's where the special, super "energy vitamin" became so important. When Pac-Man ate the energy vitamin, he became invincible. The evil ghosts could no longer harm him. Armed with that "vitamin," Pac-Man would go right through any evil that got in his path.

I realized, while reading Scripture one morning, that not only do I love Pac-Man but that I *am* Pac-Man, every time I go to Mass, every time I receive the Eucharist.

This world is a maze, filled with work to do and dangers to avoid. If I have any hope of staying alive and excelling within it, I need Christ's energy vitamin—the true flesh that brings me everlasting life, just as He promises in this verse from Saint John's Gospel.

When we don't acknowledge the evil spirits in the maze of this world around us, the devil has already won. When we don't actively pursue *the* source of life—Christ, that "energy vitamin" that keeps us going—we are cheating ourselves. The grace-filled, eucharistic "vitamin" of everlasting life is available every day if we want it.

Unlike Pac-Man, we each have only one life. Make yours count.

Salvation Given

I am the living bread which came down from heaven; if any one eats of this bread, he will live forever; and the bread which I shall give for the life of the world is my flesh.

John 6:51

To be a leader of His *pack*, I need to be a *man* willing to get in the maze, eat the "vitamin" and duke it out with evil. Game on.

Is God on IM?

Then Moses said to God, "If...they ask me, 'What is his name?' what shall I say to them?" God said to Moses, "I AM WHO I AM." And he said, "Say this to the sons of Israel, 'I AM' has sent me to you.'"

Exodus 3:13–14

SITUATION EXPLAINED

God has a message for you. Are you logged on?

SOLUTION OFFERED

I was talking with a teen on the phone the other day, but she seemed distracted. After a minute or two of short, unfocused responses, I attempted to verify my suspicion by asking her, "Are you Instant Messaging with your friends right now?"

"Um…," she paused, wanting to lie but unable to, "yes."

"How many are you messaging with?" I asked.

"Right now five; one of my friends just went offline," she offered.

Now, I know that for teens it's not only possible but also normal to have five conversations at once. To all of you teens reading this: enjoy it now. As you get older and as work, stress and jobs get busier, it gets difficult enough just talking to yourself.

Where would the world be without "IM"? Well, we'd certainly have more time on our hands to do other things. Now, *if* you read the verse (and I hope that you did), you might know where I'm going with this.

This verse recounts the moment in history when Moses, then working as a shepherd in the hills of the Midian near Mount Horeb (in case you were wondering), witnessed something miraculous: the burning bush.

You probably know how the event transpired, but if not you can always reread Exodus 3 or rent *The Prince of Egypt* (good movie, by the way). During the conversation with God, Moses asks God His name. This is the first time in the sacred Scriptures that someone is actually recorded asking God what seems to be such a simple and obvious question.

God says that His name is "I AM." An interesting side note to this is that in Hebrew the name "I AM" is spelled with the consonants *JHVH* or *YHWH,* which is where we get the names *Jehovah* and *Yahweh.*

Since God is the uncreated Creator and the unmoved Mover, the first and the last, the Alpha and the Omega (see Revelation 22:13), it seems appropriate that His name is as simple as "I AM." I mean, if someone deserves to be named simply "I AM" in this universe, it should be God, right?

Well, on this fine day the "I AM" had an "IM" of His own for Moses, a message that He wanted Moses to repeat to the pharaoh and carry to the Israelites: that they were to be freed to worship their God, this "I AM."

The beauty of this "IM" from "I AM" is that God didn't entrust the mission to five different people; He focused it on Moses. This man had the responsibility to make sure that everyone else heard the message. Moses didn't have the luxury of "IM-ing" the pharaoh either. He actually had to travel to the palace and deliver the message in person.

Moses wasn't the greatest speaker, though; he stuttered and was nervous. He eventually took his brother Aaron along to help him in that department. Still, notice that Moses didn't say, "I'm busy," or, "I'll be right back," or, "I am out to lunch," or, "I'm gonna get 'offline' now." Those responses only work on IM, not with the "I AM."

God picked one of His children for a mission. Moses replied in faith, going right away to do as the Lord had asked him to do.

God calls upon us too. He has a mission for you. He wants you to respond not at some other time but now, today. He wants you to stop and focus on His voice, listen for the message and share it with a world that desperately needs to hear of His forgiveness and love.

God is calling you, so don't change your status to "busy" or "be right back." Be present to Him. God is always "online." Don't log out, log on. He has a message that you can share with your friends and family face-to-face, not from behind a monitor.

It's your mission. Choose to accept it. Good luck.

SALVATION GIVEN

Then Moses said to God, "If...they ask me, 'What is his name?' what shall I say to them?" God said to Moses, "I AM WHO I AM." And he said, "Say this to the sons of Israel, 'I AM' has sent me to you.'"

Exodus 3:13–14

God has always used "instant messaging." It's called prayer.

Ever play cards with Jesus?

They will make war on the Lamb, and the Lamb will conquer them,
for he is Lord of lords and King of kings, and those with him are
called and chosen and faithful.

Revelation 17:14

SITUATION EXPLAINED

With Jesus as your partner, you can win at all of life's deals.

SOLUTION OFFERED

When as a kid I heard Jesus referred to as the "King of
Kings," I always thought of a card game. I pictured Jesus'
face on the "King" playing card. I know, it might sound stupid, but that's how I pictured it.

Can you imagine Jesus playing cards with the apostles? I
wonder what the *ante* would be? Please don't say,
"Elizabeth."

Remember, it all started with that *pair* in the garden.
Maybe they thought that the serpent was a *joker* (instead of
the loser that he is). Only after eating the fruit did they realize that the devil didn't know *jack*, and his lies were not
worth more than a *flush* down the toilet. We can learn something from the story of Adam and Eve, though. I mean,
while power, riches and even *diamonds* aren't forever, eternity is.

We might not feel worthy of God's love sometimes, but
we're worth more than we think, kind of like how an *ace* can
be worth one or eleven. Make no mistake, in God's mind
we're *high aces.* It's God who transforms our value by virtue
of baptism. We might "appear" the same after the sacrament, but our value has increased by His grace.

As always, our Mother Mary, the *Queen of Hearts,* is right

there praying for us and showing us how to live as perfect disciples. She knew firsthand about Jesus' birth, and through her example of discipleship, she reminds us how to live in preparation for His second coming.

The devil would have you believe that heaven is a *full house*, without room for you or me. But Jesus calls this *bluff*, reminding us that in His Father's house "there are many rooms" (John 14:2) for those who are faithful, those who repent and those who love Him.

Jesus believes in you, and He believes in me. He considers us not a *gamble* but a sure thing. He believes in our potential. Remember that in your daily *dealings*.

I don't care what the rules say; nothing beats *three of a kind*, because that's the Trinity, and the Trinity will always lead us to victory. No matter what *hand* you're *dealt*, remember that you're in His *hand* always (see Psalm 144:7).

Solution Offered

They will make war on the Lamb, and the Lamb will conquer them, for he is Lord of lords and King of kings, and those with him are called and chosen and faithful.

Revelation 17:14

I can't believe that the King of Kings knows me, little old "BG," by name, but then again,

He is a man after my own *Hart*.

It's time for me to *shuffle* off.

Be God's, everyone, for the whole game.

Notes

Chapter 2: Encountering God During Advent and Christmastime

1. Lyrics from "O Little Town of Bethlehem," written by Phillips Brooks, 1867. Music by Louis H. Redner, 1868.
2. Bill Egan, "Silent Night: The Song Heard 'Round the World," www.silentnight.web.
3. Max Lucado, *And the Angels Were Silent* (Sisters, Oreg.: Multnomah, 1999), p. 98.
4. Adapted from "Santa Claus Is Coming to Town," lyrics by Haven Gillespie; music by J. Fred Coots, 1934.

Chapter 3: Encountering God During Lent and Easter

1. Adapted from "The Bridge Operator," Wayne Rice, comp., *Hot Illustrations for Youth Talks on CD-ROM* (Grand Rapids, Mich.: Zondervan, 2001).